CONTENTS

INTRODUCTION   ix

CANTERBURY   1

DOVER   23

ISLE of THANET   51

MAIDSTONE   71

ROCHESTER   87

ROYAL TUNBRIDGE WELLS   113

SEVENOAKS   135

TENTERDEN   159

TAILPIECE – MEET the TEAM   177

INDEX of people   179

INTRODUCTION

———•———

Have you ever wished you had a knowledgeable friend willing to guide you round the places that inspired your favourite writers? If you have already read our earlier book 'Follow these Writers...in SUSSEX' you will know that this series is the answer. Each book takes you around a specific county, along main roads and off beaten tracks, down country lanes and back streets, uncovering fascinating information about writers in that area.

Charles Dickens will always be closely identified with Kent and there are many suggestions here for following him around the county he loved. Recent research has uncovered a darker side to his life (why was Mrs Dickens the only significant person not invited to her daughter's wedding near Rochester?) and this is worth exploring. Just follow the clues.

What a remarkable collection of writers come from Kent. Who would have thought that the first career choice of one of the twentieth century's greatest playwrights was as a lighthouse keeper? What a loss to drama it would have been if his application to run the North Foreland lighthouse near Broadstairs had been successful. (The Isle of Thanet chapter has his identity and the full story).

A surprising number of Kent writers led secret lives as spies. Canterbury's Christopher Marlowe died aged 29 in a 'pub brawl'. Many now believe that it was actually a 'contract killing'; the alleged double agent was becoming too unreliable. Also born near Canterbury was Aphra Behn, the first English woman to become a professional woman writer. She became a spy for Charles II.

In the twentieth century Somerset Maugham's work for HM's Secret Service is well known. Ian Fleming wrote the James Bond novels while living in St Margaret's Bay and the Dover chapter contains suggestions about following a 007 trail around Kent, many locations appearing in the novels. In fact Fleming loved the county so much he also found inspiration in it for a popular children's story which was to become an even more popular musical. Read all about that too in the Dover chapter.

Eight major centres in Kent have been selected and whichever mode of transport you choose, foot, car, bicycle or public transport, there is plenty of helpful information here to enrich your investigations.

There are suggestions for one day, two day or longer visits. Of course, it is not always possible to indulge oneself. You may be travelling with young backseat passengers who are not completely sympathetic to the idea of hunting down famous writers. There are suggestions in each chapter for child friendly places close to centres of literary pilgrimage and, who knows? This kind of detective work is highly infectious and they could easily catch the bug.

So whether you are on holiday in Kent or lucky enough to live there, use this book to find out more about the literary Men of Kent and Kentish Men (not forgetting literary Maids of Kent and Kentish Maids) who have written about the Garden of England.

Enjoy your travels.

(Note: all postcodes given are for SatNavs or other GPS devices to assist you to find the places mentioned.)

CANTERBURY

*"from every shires ende
to Caunterbury they wende"*

'Murder most foul' - it is strange how the atmosphere of intrigue and violent death hangs over this World Heritage city. It owed its fame in medieval times to the notorious murder of St. Thomas a Becket in 1170. Four hundred years later its best known son, Christopher Marlowe, was mysteriously murdered in Deptford in south London.

CANTERBURY'S WRITERS

Geoffrey Chaucer (1340-1400)

Geoffrey Chaucer spent most of his life in London, but he will always be identified with Canterbury and the poem which bears the city's name. There is some evidence that he went on a pilgrImage to Canterbury and it was possibly this which sowed the seed for 'The Canterbury Tales'. Sadly his poem was unfinished and the pilgrims never actually reached Canterbury. One would love to have had Chaucer's description of the "holy blissful martir's" shrine which, in the fourteenth century, was second only to Jerusalem and Rome as a place of pilgrimage.

'Canterbury Cathedral seen through a street entrance arch'

Chaucer lived in challenging times; he saw both the Black Death and the Peasants' Revolt. His own life too was full of drama. Aged 19, he was captured in France and ransomed, King Edward III contributing £16 towards the young squire's release. He subsequently joined the Royal Household and made many trips abroad in the king's service. It seems very likely that he passed through Canterbury frequently on his way to the Continent. He became Comptroller of the Petty Customs and was eventually created a Knight of the Shire for Kent. Perhaps it is not surprising he became such a trusted diplomat and civil servant. He was very well connected as his wife's sister, Katherine Swynford, had married John of Gaunt, the third son of King Edward III. In his spare time, Chaucer was always writing and frequently reciting his work to the court.

He died on the 25th of October 1400 and was buried in Westminster Abbey. That shows how highly he was regarded as normally this was a privilege reserved just for royalty.

Distinguished Old Boys from The King's School

Canterbury's famous school was founded by King Henry VIII and is one of the oldest in the country. Famous Old Boys range from Elizabethan playwrights John Lyly and Christopher Marlowe to Hugh Walpole and Somerset Maugham in the 1890s.

John Lyly (1554-1606)

Although less well known than many other sixteenth century poets and dramatists, John Lyly certainly deserves inclusion in any survey of that golden age of drama. He was born in Canterbury in what is now known as the Sun Inn. There was a ten year age gap between him and Christopher Marlowe so it seems unlikely their paths crossed at The King's School. After Oxford University, Lyly went off to London and made a considerable reputation for himself, writing for the newly established theatres. His best known work was probably 'Euphues - the Anatomy of Wit' and one phrase he wrote in it: "All's fair in love and war" has since entered the language.

Christopher Marlowe (1564-1593)

This Elizabethan poet and playwright packed more drama into his twenty-nine years than most people manage in a lifetime. His mysterious life, with its heady mix of theatre, religious scandal and spying, reads in part like the exciting dramas he was creating for the stage.

Christopher Marlowe, the son of a shoemaker, was born in George Street, Canterbury in 1564, one of nine children. He was two months older than his contemporary, William Shakespeare.

Aged fourteen, he became a Scholar at The King's School. He was to be awarded a further scholarship to Corpus Christi College, Cambridge.

So far, so reasonably predictable for a clever boy from the provinces but behind the scenes his actions were anything but predictable. Evidence seems to suggest that while at Cambridge he was recruited as a spy (Cambridge spies – what's new?) by Sir Francis Walsingham, Queen Elizabeth's Spymaster in Chief.

Corpus Christi College made an unsuccessful attempt to withhold Marlowe's degree as punishment for mysterious absences, even suggesting his frequent visits to the French city of Rheims were to arrange his admission to the Roman Catholic priesthood there. One can but speculate on what he was doing in the city but it seems probable that, rather than negotiating to join the Jesuits, he was actually spying on them on behalf of the English government.

Certainly a letter was received by his college from the Privy Council stating that Queen Elizabeth did not wish to see her agent penalised for serving his country. The University awarded him his Bachelor of Arts degree in 1584.

He moved to London, finding his niche in the theatrical milieu, first acting and then writing six plays of his own, which included 'Dr. Faustus' and 'Tamburlaine'. Never one to keep a low profile, Marlowe then joined Sir Walter Raleigh's atheistic School of Night circle. The sixteenth century was a dangerous time to have such views.

The playwright was accused of converting others to atheism and making fun of the Bible. He was arrested on the 18th of May 1593 but then released on bail. He clearly had some influential friends, but his luck was rapidly running out.

So, now came the final act of his amazingly dramatic life and one that is still shrouded in mystery. What is undisputed is that on the 30th of May 1593, Marlow spent the day with three men, probably fellow government agents, in a public house in Deptford. There was an argument over the bill for a meal and one of the three, Ingram Frizer, stabbed Marlowe above the right eye, killing him instantly, allegedly in self-defence. Many have suggested it was a put up job and Marlowe had been lured to Deptford by Walsingham's hirelings. The brilliant young recruit had got out of hand. The jury concluded that Frizer had acted in self-defence. He was pardoned within a month. Meanwhile, Marlowe was buried in an unmarked grave in Deptford immediately after the inquest.

Perhaps it is not surprising with all the mystery surrounding his life that his death has been an equal source of speculation. Perhaps he didn't die in the brawl. Perhaps powerful friends whisked him away to exile in Europe.

Perhaps he continued writing plays and sent them back to England under the name of William Shakespeare! Perhaps...perhaps but of all the far-fetched theories about Shakespeare's true identity (perhaps he really was the glove-maker's son from Stratford) this one does seem one of the most unlikely.

William Somerset Maugham (1875-1965)

This distinguished writer became the highest paid novelist in the world in the 1930s but in spite of his international fame he did not receive the same critical approval for his work in Britain. Sadly, this rejection, as he saw it, seemed to mirror the many other rejections which had formed his experiences from his early days.

Somerset Maugham was born in Paris, the youngest son of the solicitor to the British Embassy. His mother suffered from tuberculosis and died when he was eight years old and this was followed two years later by his father's death from cancer.

The orphan came to Kent to be brought up by his aunt and clergyman uncle, the Rev'd. Henry MacDonald Maugham, who was the vicar of Whitstable, five miles from Canterbury.

The vicarage was a source of little comfort. His uncle was cold and unfeeling and his aunt's gentler influence could not overcome the harsh regime. He was sent to The King's School in nearby Canterbury where he was teased both for his small stature and for his bad English (he was newly arrived from Paris, where French had been his first language). It is not surprising he developed a stammer there which was to remain with him for the rest of his life.

In his autobiographical novel 'Of Human Bondage' (1915), Maugham thinly disguises these experiences. He describes the childhood and early manhood of Philip Carey, born with a club foot, raised by a religious aunt and uncle, the Rev'd. William Carey, in what has now become Blackstable rather than Whitstable. The hero goes to school in Canterbury which has been renamed Tercanbury. His 1930 novel 'Cakes and Ale' is also reputed to have some material based on his life in this area.

Understandably, Maugham always said he hated his old school and yet he returned in 1961 to open the Maugham Library, which houses his own books and manuscripts of 'Liza of Lambeth' (1897) and 'Catalina' (1948).

By the age of sixteen Maugham had had enough of the school. He refused to continue his studies there and finally persuaded his uncle to allow him to leave and take what would now be called a gap year. He travelled widely in Germany before returning to Britain to train to be

5

a doctor. His early literary success meant he could quickly abandon medicine for what became a glittering literary career.

There is one curious parallel with an earlier King's Old Boy. In 1916, during the First World War, Maugham served as a British spy in Russia. Marlowe would have understood his fascination with espionage. It was to be a brief career. Maugham's stammer and poor health were considerable handicaps and after only one year he was forced to resign.

Hugh Walpole (1884-1941)

The years he spent at The King's School were the only time this prolific author spent in Kent. The son of a bishop he was born in New Zealand and came to England when five years old. A good deal of his adult life was spent in Cumberland where, amongst many other books, he wrote his best selling family saga 'The Herries Chronicle'.

Sir Patrick Leigh Fermor (1915-2011)

The author of "A Time of Gifts", popularly known as Paddy Fermor, was probably the best travel writer of his generation. He declared himself proud to have been "sacked", as he put it, from The King's School for a teenage indiscretion with a young Canterbury girl. After this his housemaster prophetically wrote that Fermor was "a dangerous mixture of sophistication and recklessness". His later life was described by a BBC journalist as "a cross between Indiana Jones, James Bond and Graham Greene".

Edmund de Waal OBE (1964-)

The author of the international best seller 'The Hare with Amber Eyes' describes himself as "a potter who writes". Whilst a pupil at The King's School his pottery teacher was Geoffrey Whiting, a disciple of Bernard Leach.

Some More Canterbury Writers

Joseph Conrad (1857-1924)

Native English readers owe this Polish born novelist a debt of gratitude for taking pity on our poor linguistic skills and anglicising his original name of **Jozef Teodor Konrad Korzeniowski**.

Conrad arrived in England, aged twenty one, in 1878 and this country then became the former merchant seaman's home. He had several homes in Kent where all his major novels were written. More will be found about him in the Tenterden chapter.

For the last four years of his life he made his home at Bishopsbourne, a small village south of Canterbury. Interestingly, this was the final home for at least two other writers, **Richard Hooker** and the naturalist and writer **Jocelyn Brooke (1908-1966)**. Conrad's funeral was held at St Thomas' R.C. church in Canterbury and he was subsequently buried in the town cemetery. His tomb bears his original Polish name.

Mary Tourtel (1874-1948) and Rupert Bear

Rupert Bear (most emphatically not Rupert *the* Bear) made his debut in the Daily Express on the 8th of November 1920. The little white bear in the yellow checked trousers and scarf was part of a Fleet Street circulation war. The 'Daily Mail' had Teddy Tail, the 'Daily Mirror' Pip, Squeak and Wilfred and the 'Daily News' Arkubs. How short lived is fame. Are any of those names recognizable today?

Mary Tourtel was born in Canterbury. She had a reputation as a professional book illustrator and was married to a sub-editor on the 'Daily Express'. He suggested that she invent a rival to Teddy Tail and the others and he in turn would produce the captions. The rest, as they say, is history.

In 1935 responsibility for both writing and illustrating the stories was assumed by **Alfred Bestall (1892-1986)**, previously an illustrator for Punch. He continued working on Rupert until well into his nineties, since when a variety of writers and artists have continued the task. Mary Tourtel spent most of her life in Canterbury and is buried in St Martin's Churchyard.

ONE DAY VISIT

Most of the major literary sites are grouped conveniently in a radius of about two miles around the cathedral but be warned. There is a lot to see.

We have given a one day itinerary but, if you want to take your time around the various exhibitions, you might find two days more comfortable.

We suggest you begin at the south of the city, close by the bus station and the new shopping precinct. There is a convenient car park in Watling Street. The house where Christopher Marlowe was born was destroyed in 1942 and Fenwicks department store now stands on the site. Turn left at the busy St. George's roundabout into St. George's Street, which changes its name first to Parade and then High Street. In front of you is the tower which is all that remains of St. George's Church. A small plaque states that Marlowe was baptised here on the 26th of February 1564. Birth certificates only date from the nineteenth century so baptism records are particularly important historical evidence. The archives in Canterbury Cathedral hold Marlowe's baptism details.

'Plaque recording Marlowe's baptism on the remains of the church tower'

Turn right at the church tower down Canterbury Lane to see St. Thomas R.C. Church on the corner of Burgate. Joseph Conrad's funeral was held here. **Richard Harris Barham (1788-1845)** was born in Burgate, although there is no record of the precise location of his house. He wrote using the *nom de plume* of **Thomas Ingoldsby** and some of his Ingoldsby Legends are set in Canterbury.

Return to the tower and continue down the High Street, turning right into Butchery Lane. Turn left at the end towards the Buttermarket. The Canterbury Visitors Centre is here with lots of helpful information.

Close by is the wooden framed Sun Hotel, built in 1503 and the home of Marlowe's contemporary from The King's School, the writer **John Lyly (1554-1606)**. Today the building has been restored by Debenhams and has become tea rooms.

There is a plaque on an outside wall giving some details of Charles Dickens' associations with this part of the city.

And now it's time to go through the imposing Christ Church Gate into the cathedral grounds. There is a charge for entrance to the grounds as well as to the cathedral itself. Founded by Saint Augustine in A.D.598, it is the oldest in the country.

The shrine of St. Thomas a Becket, murdered by four knights in the cathedral in 1179, became the most magnificent in England, covered in gold and jewels. It was originally to the east of the High Altar, in the Trinity Chapel, but that one was destroyed in 1538. **T.S. Eliot (1888-1968)** was commissioned to retell the story of Becket's martyrdom for the 1935 Canterbury Festival and his verse-play, 'Murder in the Cathedral', was first performed in the Chapter House within yards of the place where Becket was killed. The play immediately transferred to London and was certainly one of the reasons Eliot won the Nobel Prize for Literature in 1948.

In 1950 **Dorothy L. Sayers (1893-1957)**, most famous as the creator of Lord Peter Wimsey, the hero of her detective stories, was also invited to write a play for The Cathedral Festival. By now its continuing success meant it had become an annual event every October. Her play 'The Zeal of Thy House' was such a surprising success that she quickly followed it with further religious works including 'The Man Born to be King'. After that success there weren't any more detective novels.

Leave the Cathedral and go into the grounds, following the path round to the left towards the cloisters. The Canterbury Cathedral Archives are through the third entrance. The collection contains a number of documents relating to Christopher Marlowe and his family. To do some homework before your visit look up: www.canterbury-cathedral.org/histories/archives where you will find much useful information.

As you leave the Cathedral Archives turn left along the covered walkway and at the end turn left again out into the grounds of the King's School.

There are many Canterbury scenes in Charles Dickens' 'David Copperfield' and Doctor Strong's school presumably owes much to The

King's School. "A grave building in a courtyard with a learned air about it that seemed very well suited to the stray rooks and jackdaws which came down from the Cathedral towers." In 1961 Somerset Maugham endowed the school with a new library which bears his name and contains many manuscripts of his novels. Close by is Memorial Court, where the garden gate bears the emblem that he used on his novels.

It's quite a cultural shock to leave the Cathedral's peaceful environment to return to the town's hustle and bustle. Continue round the Green and go out of the gate in the far left hand corner and turn left down Palace Street. There is a wonderful crooked house on the corner, formerly the old King's School Shop, with a front door at a rickety angle to the road. It delighted Charles Dickens' sense of the absurd and he described it as: "A very old house bulging out over the road...leaning forward, trying to see who was passing on the narrow pavement below...".

'Crooked House at the corner of Palace Street'

Turn right at the Bell and Crown pub into St. Alphege Lane passing St. Alphege Church on your left. At the end of the road turn left into King Street and then take the next road on the right to The Friars.

Canterbury's most famous son, Christopher Marlowe, is

commemorated here with a recently renovated theatre named after him. Beside it is the Marlowe Memorial. Since Marlowe's Christian name was frequently abbreviated to Kit, this monument is popularly and irreverently referred to as Kitty. It's a Victorian tribute showing the main characters from four of his plays: 'Tamburlaine', 'Dr.Faustus', 'Barabas' and 'Edward II', as depicted by famous actors: Irving, Forbes Robertson, Alleyn and James Hackett.

In front of you is the High Street, again, with a wealth of literary sites whether you turn left or right. There are also plenty of restaurants to revive tired literary detectives, including the famous Weavers.

Once suitably fortified, we suggest you turn right towards Westgate. There were originally six medieval gates to the city but this is the only one which is still standing. It dates from about 1380. Had Chaucer completed 'The Canterbury Tales' his pilgrims would have entered the city here, as was the normal practice.

'West Gate'

Continue walking for about half a mile as the High Street becomes St. Dunstan's Street. Dickens used several Canterbury settings in 'David Copperfield' referring to which he said: "Of all my books I like this the best". Along St Dunstan Street you will pass the House of Agnes Hotel, which is reputed to have been the original for Agnes Wickfield's home. Dickens' stamp is all over the city, as it is over so many other Kentish places.

At the junction with London Road is St. Dunstan's Church with its poignant associations with **Thomas More (1478-1535)**, the author of 'Utopia' and hero of **Robert Bolt's** play 'A Man for all Seasons'. After her father's execution in 1535 on Tower Hill, Margaret Roper begged to be allowed to bring More's head back in a casket to her home in Canterbury. Eventually the authorities agreed and it was removed from the pole on which it had been placed outside the Tower of London.

Later, after her own death in 1577, both Margaret Roper's body and her father's severed head, in a lead casket, were interred in the recently built Roper Chapel, situated in the right hand corner of the church. There is a memorial slab on the Chapel floor. As you come out of the church look diagonally across the road to the magnificent Tudor gateway of Roper Gate. It is all that remains today of Place House, the Roper family home.

'Roper family grave and burial place of Sir Thomas More's head'

Retrace your steps back along the High Street past Westgate. The turning to The Friars and Marlowe Memorial Theatre is on your left, but now turn right down Stour Street. The Franciscan Centre is on the opposite corner with Greyfriars Guest House (01227 456255) on your right as you walk down the street. Although the Cavalier poet, **Richard Lovelace (1618-1658)** owned considerable estates, he lived here in the Dorter building when he fell on hard times under Cromwell's rule, after presenting the Kentish Petition. Today the Franciscan Garden is a peaceful oasis in the heart of the city.

Almost next door is **Rupert Bear's** very own museum and also The Museum of Canterbury, housed inside the medieval Poor Priests' Hospital. There is an interactive Marlowe exhibition where you can discover more about his life and work and investigate his mysterious death. Joseph Conrad's chair and table, at which he always wrote, are kept here and more Conrad material and books can be seen on request.

At the very end of Stour Street the road changes its name to Church Lane after St. Mildred's Church situated there. By tradition, in December 1626, **Izaak Walton (1593-1683)** (author of The Compleat Angler, published in 1653) was married in this church to Rachel Floud, the great, great niece of Archbishop Cranmer.

Make your way back towards the High Street and walk down Hawks Lane, now on your right hand side almost opposite the Rupert Bear Museum. It's a short walk. Turn left at the end into St. Margaret's Street. The Canterbury Tales Visitor Attraction will be easily seen. This amazingly vivid recreation of medieval life certainly makes you appreciate our twenty first century standard of living, as you journey through medieval Canterbury with Geoffrey Chaucer and see several of his Tales brought to life.

'Canterbury Tales Visitor Centre'

You are actually quite close to where you started at the beginning of the day. From The Canterbury Tales Visitor Attraction continue along St. Margaret Street and at the crossroads turn right into Parade. You'll see the Clock Tower in front of you and it's easy to retrace the way you came.

TWO DAY VISIT

There are two country estates, Godmersham and Goodnestone, within easy distance of Canterbury, both closely associated with **Jane Austen (1775-1817)** through her brother Edward. Unfortunately there is no simple, direct route between them so if you want to spend a pleasant day investigating the influences this area had on Jane, you will find it easiest to make two separate trips out of the city. In so doing you should also be able to take in places associated with one or two other Canterbury writers.

You may feel, however, that this involves rather too much driving. If you make a second visit to Kent with either Dover or Sandwich as your base, you could find a visit to Goodnestone easier. Make sure that you visit the correct Goodnestone. The one outside Faversham has nothing to do with Jane Austen - as far as we know.

First drive south from Canterbury to the A28 and then drive six miles southwest until you reach Godmersham, the main home of Jane's brother, Edward. He changed his surname to Austen Knight after being adopted as a boy by his cousin, the rich but childless Thomas Knight of Godmersham Park. A similar expedient is described in his sister's 1816 novel 'Emma' when Frank Churchill is also adopted, this time by a wealthy aunt. Happily, it seems likely that Edward Knight was far less snobbish than the fictional character.

In 1797, after Mr Knight's death and his widow's retirement to a house in Canterbury, Edward inherited the estate. His parents and sisters frequently visited him. "Edward excels in doing the honours to his visitors and providing for their amusement", Jane wrote home to Cassandra. On one of her earliest visits here she began writing 'First Impressions'. She later revised this earlier draft and turned it into her 1813 novel 'Pride and Prejudice'. In fact it was rumoured that she based several characters and scenes in the novel on her sharp observations around Godmersham Park. The Georgian Palladian mansion, built in 1732, is now a college for the Association of British Dispensing Opticians and so is generally closed to the public. There is, however, a public footpath running though the grounds so it is possible to view the exterior of the house from a distance.

Make sure you visit the ancient parish church, dedicated to St. Lawrence, which has one of the oldest representations of St. Thomas a Becket in the country. It was, after all, very close to the pilgrImage route. The church also has a stained glass window in the chancel and a large memorial on a wall in the nave dedicated to Edward and Elizabeth Knight. There is also a memorial to Thomas and Catherine Knight, Edward's adoptive parents.

Return to Canterbury the way you came on the A28. You will be entering the city at Harbledon, where medieval pilgrims traditionally had their first view of the city. In 'The Canterbury Tales' Chaucer gives its popular nickname of 'Bob-up-and-Down'. **Erasmus (1466-1536)**, the Dutch humanist, visited the Norman church here around 1510.

Recent research suggests that Harbledon was the birthplace of

Aphra Behn (1640-1689) although Anne Finch, Countess of Winchilsea assigned her birthplace a few miles further south in Wye. Aphra Behn was the first Englishwoman to become a professional writer and had an amazingly colourful life.

Her father was appointed Lieutenant Governor of Surinam. Living for several years in South America gave her much useful material for her novel 'Orinoko or the Royal Slave'. Her husband is thought to have been a London merchant who died in 1665, probably from plague.

She became a spy for Charles II, probably in Holland. (The Canterbury air certainly seems to encourage espionage. Christopher Marlowe and Somerset Maugham's double lives are well documented, while in nearby St Margaret's Bay, Dover, Ian Fleming was busy creating 007 - James Bond). Aphra Behn's paymasters were so dilatory that she spent some time in a debtors' prison. Her writing, especially plays such as 'The Rover' and 'The City Heiress', brought great critical acclaim in her lifetime and she was buried in Westminster Abbey.

Take the A290 out of the city. From Canterbury it is eight miles north to Whitstable, where Somerset Maugham's cold hearted uncle had his vicarage. The road passes through Blean, the medieval Forest of Blean. Not far from here (at what is now called Boughton Street) Chaucer's pilgrims were joined by a canon's yeoman.

After about five miles the road becomes the B2205.On the outskirts of Whitstable turn right into Sadleton Road (A290). On the right hand side is Forge Lane. The Maugham vicarage stood here but has now been demolished to make way for flats in Maugham Court.

Somerset Maugham's uncle was Vicar of All Saints Church to be found, inevitably, in Church Street (CT5 1PG). From Maugham Court turn left to rejoin the Canterbury Road and drive towards the railway station. Turn right into Belmont Road. Church Street leads off this.

The Church grounds are an oasis of calm, one feels deep in the countryside rather than in a busy seaside resort. There is a helpful plan of the church grounds in the car park indicating where Henry MacDonald Maugham is buried.

Make your way to the war memorial behind the church and with your back to the church the grave is a short distance to your left, just inside the small wooded area. If you want to look inside the church make sure you are there between 10.00am and 12.00noon on a Saturday, when it is open for visitors. The pulpit is worth noticing as it was given by the Rev'd. MacDonald Maugham in memory of his wife.

It has been another very full day but if you feel you can fit in more sightseeing, especially if you want to continue the Jane Austen trail, take the A257 south east for Goodnestone (CT3 1PL). If you have to stop to ask for directions remember it's pronounced 'Gunstone'. At Wingham turn right at the Red Lion pub onto the B2046 and after one mile turn left and follow all signs to Goodnestone Park Gardens. In 1791 Jane's brother, Edward, married Elizabeth Bridges, who was the daughter of the estate owner and the couple lived on the estate at Rowling House. Jane spent several holidays here and mentions in her letters leading the dancing at the evening parties at The Park. Two hundred years later the fourteen acres are still exquisite ("A haven of beautiful tranquillity" said Ursula Buchan writing in the 'Daily Telegraph') but it would be a good idea to confirm the opening times beforehand. Website: www.goodnestoneparkgarden.co.uk or telephone 01304 840107

Generally the gardens are closed all day on Saturday and Monday and open afternoons only in the summer months. Whatever else you do make sure that you also make your way to the tea room. The cakes are freshly made, without any preservatives being used.

Before you leave Goodnestone you should go and see the parish church. The antiquarian and short story writer **M.R. James (1862-1936)** - always known by his initials but it's actually Montague Rhodes James - was born in the rectory and baptized in the church.

IF YOU HAVE MORE TIME

Follow the Pilgrims' Way

In the Middle Ages there were several well-trodden pilgrImage routes from all points of the compass to Canterbury. During the course of the previous two days you have covered some of the final part of the principal route from London through North Kent. With more time you might like to trace this route in its entirety. Chaucer refers to several stopping places in 'The Canterbury Tales' and from these clues it is possible to work out the probable order for the various Tales. Don't be put off by Chaucer's English. There are many 'easy to read' modern versions available. In our opinion Nevill Coghill's is certainly the best.

Southwark ("in Southwerk as I lay") was a popular meeting place in London for pilgrims gathering together for the 54 mile journey. Inns, such as Harry Bailey's Tabard Inn, did a good trade. They frequently offered an all inclusive package tour with horses for the journey, a bed for the night and, as in this case, a guide for the trip. From there it was about a four day ride to the shrine.

The Pilgrims' Way follows Watling Street, the main Roman road to Canterbury. If you drive along the A2 you will be close to it.

Chaucer's pilgrims leave Southwark at daybreak following today's Old Kent Road .They make their first stop outside London at St. Thomas' Watering Place.

> "And off we rode at slightly faster pace
> Than walking to St. Thomas' watering-place"

This was a small stream where horses were watered, about a half hour's ride from the Tabard. Here the Knight tells the first tale. You are more likely to be filling up with petrol today than looking after your horses. Traditionally the site is between 509 and 511 Old Kent Road.

The route continues through Deptford and Blackheath. In the Prologue to the Reeve's Tale, Harry Bailey, the self-appointed Master of Ceremonies on the journey, says:

> "Why, look! Here's Deptford and its nine o'clock!
> And Greenwich too, with many a blackguard in it"

After riding through Welling and Dartford (where many pilgrims spent their first night), the motley crowd reach Rochester and it's the Monk's turn to entertain the rest.

> "For it's your turn to tell a story, sir.
> Why, look! We've almost got to Rochester!"

The second night of a pilgrImage was often spent here at the half way point, possibly at The Crown Inn built in 1316. Its later namesake stands on the same spot. Pilgrims could use the opportunity to hire fresh horses. Each of the two sections of the journey cost 12 pence and the horses' flanks were clearly branded so there was little chance of riders absconding with them.

In the fourteenth century the road rose towards the hills of Blean Forest. The village of Boughton was on the west side. Before this steep climb, five miles beyond Sittingbourne, Chaucer's pilgrims were suddenly joined by the Canon's Yeoman.

> "Some five miles further on, as I suppose,
> At Boughton-under Blean we saw a hack
> Come galloping up".

After Boughton Street, as it is now called, the route passes through Upper Harbledon, then through a valley towards "a little town". Today it is known as Harbledon but Chaucer quaintly refers to it as "Bob-up-and-down".

> "Don't you all know where stands a little town
> The one that people call Bob-up-and-down
> Near Blean Woods on the way to Canterbury?"

Chaucer's cook has fallen asleep in the saddle.

> "What's up with you to sleep this sunny morrow?
> Have you had fleas all night or else got drunk?"

With the unhygienic sleeping arrangements in the inns at the time, including sackcloth beds stuffed with hay and sharing with complete strangers, it is quite possible the former was the reason. Probably many of Chaucer's listeners would have nodded their heads ruefully, remembering similar experiences.

Although Chaucer's intention had been to give each pilgrim two stories to tell on the way to Canterbury and two on the way back, he did not come anywhere near completing this ambitious project. We leave them at Harbledon and can only imagine them crossing the river Stour and entering Canterbury through the West Gate.

CAN I DO THESE TOURS WITHOUT A CAR?

Yes. Travelling to and from Canterbury is certainly easy with a car, thanks to those Roman builders for the original long straight roads. There are many 'greener' ways to travel which could mean you see most of the significant sites without the hassle of looking for parking places.

There are two mainline railway stations in the city: Canterbury East and Canterbury West, with frequent trains from London Victoria. Journey time is approximately 90 minutes. If you are travelling from the European mainland on Eurostar you will find an easy connection at Ashford International station with a journey time of 20 minutes to Canterbury. Whitstable is also on a direct line from London Victoria (that journey time is approximately 80 minutes). For further information on these and other journeys contact National Rail Enquiries on +44 (0) 8457 484 950

The area is well served by buses from Stagecoach East Kent (you need the Nos. 4, 4A, 4B or 5 if you are travelling between Canterbury and Whitstable). Much more information is available on 08717 818181 or go to the web site: www.nationalexpress.com

Finally, for the really fit, you could get on your bike to tackle the many safe cycle routes in the area, especially the ride to Whitstable along part of the famous Crab and Winkle Line. All the cycling information you need is on 'Spokes' on 01227 738 296

BEST TIME TO VISIT

One of the nicest times to visit the city is for the two weeks every October when the Kent International Festival of Arts takes place in and around Canterbury.

It's been running since the 1920s with one of its most significant years being 1935, when T.S. Eliot's specially commissioned play 'Murder in the Cathedral' was first performed. There is always a mixed programme of literature, drama, music, dance, cinema and visual arts on offer.

IF YOU HAVE CHILDREN

Depending on the age of the children there are two exhibitions in Canterbury which are child heaven. While you are immersed in Marlowe and Conrad memorabilia in the Canterbury Heritage Museum, young children will love to visit the Rupert Bear Museum (more information on 01227 475202 or www.canterbury-museums.co.uk) in the next door building, with its interactive exhibits. It's open all year round.

For big kids of all ages The Canterbury Tales visitor attraction (for information telephone 01227 479227 or www.canterburytales.org.uk) cannot be beaten for an introduction to the sights sounds and smells of the Middle Ages as well, of course, to some of Chaucer's best known tales recreated in dramatic form.

All this sightseeing can be tiring and the award winning Canterbury Historic River Tours could be just the answer for those tired feet.

The tour has won many awards for the way it combines a light hearted commentary whilst discovering some of Canterbury's loveliest architecture. Telephone for info on 07790 534744 or try www. canterburyrivertours.co.uk

'River Tours boats landing site'

You might also find it helpful to stop off at Wingham Wildlife Park (CT3 1JL) on your way to Goodnestone Gardens. It's open every day except Christmas Day and Boxing Day but the web site will give you all the details: www.winghamwildlifepark.co.uk or call 01227 720836.

DOVER
Iconic White Cliffs

———◆———

The 300 feet high White Cliffs of Dover have always been a sign of home for travellers, arousing patriotism and nostalgia in equal measure. In 1942, during World War II, this became particularly true when Dame Vera Lynn addressed the nation's hopes and fears in her song 'There'll be Bluebirds over the White Cliffs of Dover'. (Bluebirds? Off the Kent coast?)

It is said that bluebirds had to be substituted for the more plausible seagulls since they didn't fit the music but it may also be no coincidence that the composer and librettist were both American. It became one of the most popular World War II songs and raised a weary nation's morale after the Battle of Britain.

DOVER'S WRITERS

Lord Byron (1788-1824)

"Mad, bad and dangerous to know", famously said Lady Caroline Lamb of her charismatic lover. To those epithets one could add "and endlessly fascinating". So many places would like a share in his fame. Byron is

The great attraction of this area for Fleming was Royal St.George's Golf Club at Sandwich and perhaps the proudest moment of his life was his election as captain of the club for 1964/5. He was present at a committee meeting on 11 August 1964 when he suffered a heart attack. He died in Canterbury the following day and is buried near his final home in Wiltshire.

ONE DAY VISIT

For centuries Dover's majestic cliffs formed the first line of defence against invasion from Europe. The port became known as 'the Key to England' and by Royal Charter in 1260 along with Hastings, Romney, Hythe and Sandwich became one of the Confederation of Cinque Ports.

These five 'head ports' each provided the Crown with 57 ships and crew for 15 days every year. Privileges came from this service. There was freedom from some taxes and duties and exemption from the jurisdiction of external courts. After 500 years a permanent English fleet was established in the 16th century and the need for ship service faded away.

France is fewer than 20 miles away at the closest point from this 'Gateway to Europe' and on a busy day the port can process up to 10,000 freight vehicles and just over 200 coaches. But amid all the hurly-burly it is still possible to track down much of the town's literary past. Almost all the sites, perhaps inevitably given the town's history, are close to the waterfront.

Did William Shakespeare come here? There is no concrete evidence for this but, if he did go to Europe in those 'lost years' before he suddenly appeared on the London theatrical scene, then it is very likely he would have crossed from Dover. The description of the dizzy view from the "high and unbending cliff" in Act 4 of King Lear, as the blind and despairing Gloucester attempts suicide in "the country near Dover" has the real feel of personal observation about it – not to be gained in the playwright's home town. Stratford upon Avon is about as far as you can get from the sea in England.

'Cliffs at Samphire Hoe'

Shakespeare Cliff is on the west of the town and makes a good starting point. From the A20 follow directions to the Western Heights and Samphire Hoe Coastal Country Park (Edgar had described his view of the cliff: "half way down/ hangs one that gathers samphire - dreadful trade"). Close to the cliff is a subway to the beach with an excellent view up to the cliff side. For more information on this area visit www. samphirehoe.com. The Western Heights has been designated part of the Kent Downs Area of Outstanding Natural Beauty (AONB) and for more about this contact 01622 2215222 or www.kentdowns.org.uk

From this lonely spot rejoin the twenty first century by driving along the A20 to Dover. In 1851 **Mathew Arnold (1822-1888)** and his bride spent some days after their June wedding here at The Lord Warden Hotel, where he probably wrote 'Dover Beach'. It is also possible the poem was composed on the way back from their continental honeymoon when the couple also stayed in Dover. Either way, it is easy to imagine Arnold beckoning his wife to the window to see the calm view with the moonlight on the water:

> "on the French coast the light
> Gleams and is gone; the cliffs of England stand
> Glittering and vast, out in the tranquil bay".

The whole poem becomes a metaphor for the many challenges to traditional beliefs in the nineteenth century. Arnold contrasts the reassuring permanence of nature seen in the strength of the cliffs, the predictability of the waves and the changing intellectual certainties of his own day. For the sake of pleasant sightseeing, we trust that it is a tranquil day for you on your visit and no stormy weather.

The Lord Warden Hotel was one of the first purpose built railway hotels to be constructed after the rail connection with London was established in 1844. It is still there as a building but now it is used as offices and known as Lord Warden House. Because of its proximity to Dover Station it became a convenient overnight stopping place for travellers waiting to embark for France. The exiled Napoleon III, **George Eliot, William Makepeace Thackeray** and **Charles Dickens** all stayed here. It can clearly be seen at the entrance to Admiralty Pier.

Continue your journey eastward to the town. Charles Dickens and Wilkie Collins both stayed at Number 10 Camden Crescent (CT16 1LE) in 1852 and this is commemorated by a blue plaque, although much of the terrace was destroyed by bombing during World War II. This was inevitably the case with a good deal of historic Dover.

'Camden Terrace with plaque for Charles Dickens and Wilkie Collins'

Just outside Dover is a plethora of literary sites. Drive four miles along the coast to St.Margaret's Bay (CT15 6EF). This former fishing village became the seaside resort of choice for many of the rich and famous from late Victorian times. More recently, in the 1930s, Edith Nesbit, author of 'The Railway Children', bought a house here and the area became even more fashionable in 1945 when Noel Coward moved in. He knew Kent well and had a house in Romney Marsh (part of Day Two's visit) which had been requisitioned by the army during World War II.

Extensive restoration was needed for it at the end of the war. Coward needed somewhere else to live - a bolt hole from London - and fell in love instantly with White Cliffs, a white house with a red roof and lime-green shutters on the far north end of St. Margaret Bay's shingle beach. His housing arrangements were still not perfect. British and Canadian troops had trained for D Day here and they had torn the place apart.

There was no heating or light and the wind whistled through the broken open windows. But the setting was wonderful, built so close to the sea that waves lapped the bedroom walls and Coward said: "I don't think I can fail to be happy here". And happy he was, at the height of his writing and performing power. The six years he spent at White Cliffs saw the creation of many outstanding plays including 'Blithe Spirit' and 'Brief Encounter'.

'White Cliffs'

After six very happy years here, Coward sold the house in 1952 to his friend, and neighbour in Jamaica, Ian Fleming. The time that Fleming spent in St Margaret's Bay was to be crucial to the James Bond stories. He spent (very) long weekends here and set at least two novels: 'Moonraker' and 'Goldfinger' in this area. Even the 007 tag had a local inspiration since it was the number of the London to Dover mail coach. Today the National Express service from London Victoria to Deal has the same iconic number.

Try to make time to visit The Pines Visitor Centre and Museum (CT15 6DZ) close by on Beach Road. The museum has some fascinating displays about local history, including much information about both Noel Coward and Ian Fleming. If it is lunchtime now you may be glad of the appetizing sandwiches and cakes served in the tea room. Check visiting times beforehand on www.pinesgarden.co.uk or call 01304 851737.

'Pines Gardens'

Delicious lunch is also available at the Coastguard pub and restaurant situated right on St. Margaret's Bay - as its publicity intriguingly states "when the English Channel is about to wet your toes, you'll be there". Ring 01304 853176 or visit www.thecoastguard.co.uk for more details.

An afternoon on the 007 trail

And now well fortified we suggest you follow in the footsteps of James Bond. So many settings in the novels come from near here. You may first like to follow the cliff top walk between St. Margaret's Bay and Kingsdown. Sir Hugo Drax's 'Moonraker' research establishment is almost certainly located in this area "on the edge of the cliffs between Dover and Deal". There are lyrical descriptions of the view. "The carpet of green turf, bright with small wildflowers, sloped down to the long beaches of Walmer and Deal. It was a panorama full of colour and excitement and romance".

Great care is needed exploring here. The chalk is unstable and it is surprising that both James Bond and Gala Brand survived the landslide which Sir Hugo Drax engineered on the cliffs. Go to www.baytrust.org.uk for more advice on walking in the area. You may, however, decide that a much easier way is to get back in the car and drive north along the A258, making a brief diversion to Kingsdown. Probably Fleming imagined Drax's house as one of those beside Kingsdown Golf Course. There is a steep cliff path at Oldstairs Bay which leads down from the golf course.

Continue along the A258 north west to Sandwich (CT13 9PB) for a different golf course, the one which first brought Fleming to this area. The Royal St. George's Golf Club at Sandwich has been the venue for the British Open Golf Championship many times. From the 1930s Fleming spent weekends playing at what he described in 'Goldfinger' as "the greatest seaside golf course in the world", staying at Guilford Hotel, Sandwich Bay (now demolished) before he bought White Cliffs. He would drive down on a Friday afternoon in time for 9 or 18 holes before tea and of course a dry martini in the clubhouse. As we noted earlier, he was elected captain for 1964/5 and attended a committee meeting on 11 August 1964. He suffered a severe heart attack and died in Canterbury the next day.

Renamed Royal St. Mark's, his beloved golf course became the setting "on a beautiful day in May with larks singing" for the tense match between Bond and Auric Goldfinger who gave his name to the 1959 novel. Hole for hole Fleming describes the Royal St George's course.

Of course 007 wins and with his usual sang-froid is even able to take his eyes off the game long enough to gaze "at the glittering distant sea and at the faraway crescent of white cliffs beyond Pegwell Bay". The golf course itself is the club's private property but there is a public footpath across the course from the town of Sandwich to the sea. You should be able to trace the game from the path.

'Royal St.George's Clubhouse'

If time allows, make sure you spend some time in Sandwich. It has attracted many writers, including **Daniel Defoe (c.1660-1731)**. He passed through the town in 1722 and recounted his experiences in 'A Tour through the Whole Isle of Great Britain'. Sadly it made a poor impression on him: "an old decayed port, miserable town". Nearly forty years later the radical thinker **Tom Paine (1737-1809)** spent all of 1759 lodging at 20 New Street (no longer there) trying to make a living as a stay maker. The author of 'The Rights of Man' was to have a strong influence on the wording of The American Declaration of Independence. And in the twentieth century **W.W. Jacobs (1863-1943)** used Sandwich, disguising its name slightly, as his inspiration for his 1902 novel 'At Sunwich Port'. More recently, **Paul Theroux (1941-)** was most complimentary and, in our view, most accurate about the charm of the town in his 1982 book 'The Kingdom by the Sea', summing it up as "pretty and still old fangled".

The pretty old-fangled town has one other attraction worth looking out for – The Secret Gardens of Sandwich. These are the ornamental gardens around The Salutation, the Grade 1 listed manor house designed by Sir Edwin Lutyens. The gardens are lovely at any time of the year but the 10,000 daffodils which bloom throughout March are particularly beautiful. For more information call 01304 619919 or visit www.the-secretgardens.co.uk

After that diversion, pick up the 007 trail again. From Sandwich take the A257 to Canterbury, turning off at Wingham onto the B2046 and then following signs to Bekesbourne. Next to the church is The Old Palace (CT4 5ES) which, after White Cliffs, became Fleming's rather smart bolthole for long golfing weekends with his wife Ann and son Caspar. It may not have been a wise move. A palace sounds very grand, although this one is an eight bedroom eighteenth century construct. Ann Fleming did not like it any better than she had liked windswept White Cliffs. She told her friends it was a wretched house and far too near the railway line.

It was to be Fleming's last permanent home in Kent. The family moved to Wiltshire, although he continued to rent property at different times in Pegwell Bay and Sandwich. Nothing could separate him from his beloved Royal St.George's.

South of the Old Palace, just off the A20, east of Bridge, is Higham Park (CT4 5BE). This was once home to Count Louis Zborowski, a colourful millionaire who designed and built cars with aeroplane engines fitted onto automobile chassis. He named at least four of them in succession Chitty, Bang and Bang (Yes! just the one 'Chitty' originally) and amazed the local population by road testing his prototype cars along the A2. Fleming was quite a jackdaw when it came to sourcing his novels and this was almost too good to be true.

He visited Higham Park sometime after the Count's death on the racing circuit and incorporated some of the legendary accounts into his children's story 'Chitty Chitty Bang Bang', originally written for his son Caspar. Higham Park, a neo classical house, has recently undergone extensive restoration and is now largely used for private functions although it is occasionally open to the public. More information is available by telephoning 01227 830830.

A short distance south from Bridge is Pett Bottom (CT4 5PB), a special place for James Bond enthusiasts. In chapter 21 of 'You Only Live

Twice' (1964) Bond is missing, presumed dead on a secret mission to Japan. His boss, M, writes a detailed obituary for The Times newspaper. There is some invaluable information here for all 007 researchers. "When he was eleven years of age both his parents were killed in a climbing accident in Chamonix and the youth came under the guardianship of an aunt, since deceased, Miss Charmian Bond, and went to live with her at the quaintly named hamlet of Pett Bottom, near Canterbury in Kent. There, in a small cottage hard by the attractive Duck Inn, his aunt, who must have been a most erudite and accomplished lady, completed his education and he passed satisfactorily into Eton."

The above is a compliment to what was in reality one of Fleming's favourite pubs. He even had his favourite seat in its picturesque garden and a blue plaque at the front of the building states that 'You Only Live Twice' was written here in 1964. Miss Charmian Bond's imagined cottage actually forms part of the pub.

Fleming was right, the Duck Inn makes a good refreshment stop. Call 01227 830354 for more information (and, of course, reports of Bond's death were greatly exaggerated and he lived to have many more nail biting adventures).

'Pett Bottom – Duck Inn with a plaque on its wall'

The quickest way back to Dover is along the A2, turning off at Lydden to follow the old road into Dover. It's the route that Bond followed in 'Moonraker': "He concentrated on his driving as he coasted down into Dover. He kept left and was soon climbing out of the town again past the wonderful cardboard castle."

You may be hopeful that you can track down the original of Bond's Café Royal in Dover. "In Dover Bond pulled up at the Café Royal, a modest little restaurant with a modest kitchen but capable, as he knew of old, of turning out excellent fish and egg dishes. The Italian-Swiss mother and son who ran it welcomed him as an old friend." Fleming enjoyed eating at the Royal Café (another one of those barely disguised names) on Bench Street, its owners too were Italian-Swiss, but since his day there has been considerable redevelopment of the area and sadly the original is no longer there. Instead it is now the entrance to a youth training scheme. One can speculate too whether the Royal Café inspired the title of Fleming's first book 'Casino Royale'.

We suggest you head down to the ferry terminal (CT17 9DQ) at the harbour for your final visit of the day. This was the location for filming scenes in the 1971 movie: 'Diamonds Are Forever' where Bond outwits Peter Franks, a diamond smuggler, at passport control and boards a hovercraft bound for Amsterdam in his place.

TWO DAY VISIT

Day Two sees us first driving seven miles west of Dover along the A259 to nearby Folkestone. Charles Dickens came here many times. From 1862 he seems to have used it as a base to visit his mistress, the actress Ellen Ternan, who was living in Northern France. She had to be sufficiently distant from England and the danger of tainting Dickens' wholesome reputation.

He had, though, first come to Folkestone nine years earlier in 1853, staying for a few days holiday at the Pavilion Hotel. His sons were at boarding school in Boulogne so this was a perfect base for the cross channel packet service. In the summer of 1855 he returned, renting No.3 Albion Villas: "a pleasant little house with the sea below and the scent of thyme sweetening the breezes from the downs". He was working very hard on 'Little Dorrit' and although it was school holiday time for his eight children, who were all staying in the house, it was not a carefree time for him. As always he had a strict routine. He spent five hours writing between nine and two every day, after which he walked alone until five in the afternoon.

One imagines the children actually saw very little of their father. Certainly he complained to friends that they were noisy and that this distracted him. Things quietened down at the beginning of September, when 8 year old Sydney was sent to boarding school in Boulogne to join his big brothers, 11 year old Frank and 10 year old Alfred. Since 13 year old Walter had left Folkestone in August to start training for the Indian Army (children had to grow up quickly in Victorian England!) Dickens finally had much more of the peace and quiet he wanted to devote to his writing.

No.3 Albion Villas is now called Copperfield House. Although David Copperfield did memorably walk to Dover, one feels a reference to 'Little Dorrit' would be more appropriate, as that was the novel written here. There is a blue plaque attached to what is now a Nursing Home marking Dickens' stay. You'll find it in a private road close to the war memorial at the eastern end of the Road of Remembrance (CT20 1SZ). In summer months it would be pleasant to park on the esplanade to take the funicular railway up the cliff side to this elegant area, known as The Leas Promenade.

'Albion Villas with a plaque by the small front window'

Return to the A259 to drive to nearby Sandgate, virtually a suburb of Folkestone. It has seen many literary visitors over the years. In late 1896 **H.G. Wells** was visiting New Romney in the forlorn hope that the sea air would be beneficial for his poor health. He chanced upon Sandgate, fell in love with its charm and went on to live in the town for the next thirteen years. His health dramatically improved and Sandgate saw the birth of many of his major novels, including 'Kipps' in 1905 and 'The History of Mr.Polly' in 1910.

Wells lived in three different houses here. Initially he and his wife rented Beach Cottage on the corner of Granville Road East and Granville Parade (CT20 3AL). If you want to stretch your legs for a bracing walk on the sea front follow signs to Castle Road Car Park. The views from Beach Cottage are stunning but as the name suggests it is situated right on the beach, there is even a lifebuoy on the outside. In 1896 there was no breakwater and in bad weather the waves broke right over the roof.

'Beach Cottage with a plaque on the wall and the Castle Road house'

There was a quick move to a nearby semi-detached villa, Arnold House, 20 Castle Road (CT20 3AG). Wells' literary career had taken off by now and from Arnold House he was able to supervise the building of Spade House (the unusual name reflects the distinctive decorations in the brickwork) in a commanding position overlooking the terraced gardens down to Sandgate Bay. It was specifically designed for him by the eminent

Arts and Crafts architect C.F. Voysey. Both writer and architect seem to have preferred their initials to their first names! At first he used a small study for writing but as his output and his popularity increased he enlarged it and then built a garden study where he could be undisturbed.

Much of Wells' time was spent socializing with the many writers who had settled in and around nearby Romney Marsh. But in 1909 there was a very public quarrel with **Henry James**, who was living in Rye, just over the border in East Sussex. After this Wells finished the book he was working on, 'Tono-Bungay', and then immediately left Sandgate, taking his family to London, never to return. The year before he had published 'The War in the Air', which was to prove prophetic. Nine years later, in May 1917, Folkestone became the first town to experience aerial bombardment.

You won't find Spade House on any map today, instead it has been renamed Wells House (CT20 2JQ). The large building in Radnor Cliff Crescent, with its glorious views over the channel, is now a nursing home with the gateway sporting two plaques indicating its former owner. Along with the more usual blue plaque is an impressively carved stone open book commemorating Wells' stay here – and here the earlier name of Spade House is used.

'Plaque showing an open book at Spade (now Wells) House'

Sandgate has been a temporary home to many other literary figures. In 1790 the leading tragic actress of her age, **Sarah Siddons (1755-1831)** returned from a visit to France where her daughters were being educated. It was a rough crossing to Dover and on landing she immediately made her way to the peace of Sandgate. She told a friend "It is the most agreeable sea place, excepting those on the Devonshire coast, I ever saw. At present the place cannot contain above twenty or thirty strangers, I should think. I have bathed four times and I believe I shall persevere on."

In 1813 Fanny Burney managed to escape from France during a lull in the fighting; it was still two years until Napoleon's defeat at Waterloo. She spent time with her brother, Charles, and his family who were residents here. As she came out of Folkestone Parish Church she was introduced to the great reformer William Wilberforce. Twenty years later, in 1832 Mary Shelley, author of Frankenstein, took up lodgings in the town to avoid the cholera epidemic that was sweeping through London at that time.

But it was H.G.Wells' twelve year residence which saw the greatest influx of writers. **Arnold Bennett, J.M. Barrie, John Galsworthy, Hilaire Belloc** and **George Bernard Shaw** all were frequently entertained by Wells at Spade House, which became in those few years one of the most important literary centres in the country.

The trail now takes us westward into Romney Marsh and very different scenery from those seaside views. This strange lonely landscape, first reclaimed from the sea by the Romans, is really several marshes, frequently deserted except for the famous sheep. Its very isolation, fearsome to many, has been attractive to several writers in need of peace and quiet as well as others with much more dubious reasons for living off the beaten track. The Marsh has long been a centre for smuggling and Rudyard Kipling's words on Romney Marsh's 'cottage industry' are famous:

"Five and twenty ponies
Trotting through the dark
Brandy for the Parson
Baccy for the Clerk;
Laces for a lady, letters for a spy,
And watch the wall my darling, while the Gentlemen go by!"

It sounds very romantic but in reality it was a rough trade and could frequently be sickeningly brutal.

From Folkestone continue on the A259 through Hythe to Dymchurch. Here we are on the trail of the fictional Dr.Syn (alias The Scarecrow) who was a well-respected vicar by day and a notorious smuggler by night. The first story was published in 1915 but the setting is 18th century Romney Marsh.

Syn's creator, the actor and novelist **Russell Thorndike (1885-1972)**, was a frequent visitor to Dymchurch, writing many of the stories in a lifeboat cottage by the sea wall (it has since been demolished).

Dr.Syn was probably created 3000 miles away in Carolina, USA. Russell Thorndyke and his sister Sybil were touring America with a theatrical company when a murder took place outside their hotel. The victim's body was left all night on the sidewalk below their balcony window. (Now there's material for a frightening story!) They were both so overwrought that they could not sleep and instead sat up all night making up adventure stories set in the area they both knew well.

They had been brought up in Kent, living close to Rochester Cathedral, when their father was appointed a canon (see the Rochester chapter for more about their childhood). Although Dr.Syn is a fictional character, many of his murderous gang's actions are based on real life incidents.

'Dr.Syn signs at the Ship Inn plus gallows and gibbet'

The Ship Inn (TN22 0NS) (01303 872122), in the High Street opposite the church, was the headquarters in the stories for the 'Marsh Men', the fictional Dr.Syn's band of smugglers.

With its extensive underground passages it was certainly used in real life by smugglers in the eighteenth and early nineteenth centuries. Today it is a warm welcoming spot serving delicious traditional pub food. There are fascinating wall displays relating to Thorndike and his smuggling stories as well as the 1960 Walt Disney film based on them. Have a look at the inn's website for more information: www.shipinn. biz.

Across the road from the inn is the village church of St. Peter and St. Paul. There is a brass plaque here commemorating Russell Thorndike. If you are a fan of the stories you will realise that many of the characters' names came from the gravestones in the churchyard. Interestingly, in 1960 the Walt Disney version of 'Dr.Syn' was not filmed here but in the church at Old Romney. This was felt to be a more authentic church setting since, after restoration work, the Dymchurch one was no longer as described in the novel.

Rejoin the A259 and drive south west along the coast for two miles to St Mary's Bay, turning right where signposted to St Mary in the Marsh. Just before the railway line is Nesbit Road, named after **Edith Nesbit (1858-1924)**. She and her second husband, Thomas Tucker, nicknamed 'The Skipper' because of his naval connections, lived in The Long Boat, a small house at the end of this road in what was then only a tiny hamlet. It was known then (and still is by many locals) as Jesson St. Mary (TN29 0SF).

Continue to St. Mary in the Marsh with its lovely old church, parts of which date back to Norman times (TN29 0BX). In the churchyard is a copy of the simple memorial to Edith Nesbit, carved by her husband, and consisting of two wooden posts with a rail across the top in an H shape. The original became badly weathered and is now inside the church. Also inside the church on the south wall above the font is a memorial plaque to the writer. Placed there by her many friends, it recalls that Edith Nesbit "delighted the hearts of so many children by her books".

'House where Edith Nesbit lived and plaque by the front door'

As you come out of the church look across to the Star Inn. The young Noel Coward lived in a small cottage next to the inn and wrote his earliest plays here. He was a great admirer of Edith Nesbit's work and even when he died a copy her story 'The Enchanted Castle' was beside his bed. Later on this tour we shall see his next, much more imposing, home on the marsh.

The next port of call is Brenzett to the north west (TN29). Much depends on your navigational skills in this challenging countryside. The easy way is to return the way you came to St. Mary's Bay and pick up the A259 again to take you through New Romney to Brenzett. The potentially more exciting route is through the lanes. If you stick to roads directing you to Ivychurch you shouldn't have any problems.

Edith Nesbit had been fascinated by Romney Marsh for many years before she and 'The Skipper' moved here and perhaps one of her best ghost stories, 'Man-size in Marble', is set on Hallowe'en at Brenzett church.

A hundred years earlier **William Cobbett (1763-1835)** travelled across Romney Marsh on horseback recounting his experiences in his book 'Rural Rides' published in 1830. He was underwhelmed by his reception. "At Breznett I with great difficulty got a rasher of bacon for breakfast. The few houses that there are, are miserable in the extreme. The church here large and nobody to go to it. What! Will the vagabonds attempt to make us believe that these churches were built for nothing?" Of course it is entirely possible that Cobbett's frosty reception was because the villagers were busy stowing away the latest hoard of smuggled spirits!

Continue north along the A2070 following directions to Hamstreet and turn off along the B2067 to Warehorne church (TN26 2LJ), Cobbett's route in reverse. **Richard Harris Barham (1788-1845)** was appointed rector of nearby Snargate and Warehorne in 1817. Two years later the gig he was travelling in overturned and he suffered a broken leg. He was forced to rest in the red-brick rectory (now Church Farm) next to the church and made good use of the time by starting to write 'The Ingoldsby Legends', using the pseudonym Thomas Ingoldsby of Tappington Manor.

The stories and poems (the best known is probably 'The Jackdaw of Rheims') were all set in the Middle Ages, but there was also plenty of drama going on around the rectory in Barham's time. The church and the nearby Woolpack Inn are linked together by a tunnel built by smugglers. It seems inconceivable that the good rector didn't know anything about it. Sadly for Romney Marsh, he was appointed a minor canon of St. Paul's Cathedral in 1821. He left the area and never returned.

The 'Ingoldsby Legends' were published in monthly episodes between 1837 and 1844 in 'Mr.Bentley's Miscellany'. They enjoyed huge success. If you are following this trail in gloomy wintry weather (perhaps not the most advisable time to drive round the marsh) think about what he said in one of the most famous tales, 'The Leech of Folkestone'. "The world, according to the best geographers is divided into Europe, Asia, Africa, America and Romney Marsh. In this last named and fifth quarter of the globe, a witch may still be occasionally discovered in favourable, i.e. stormy seasons, weathering Dungeness Point in an egg shell or careering on her broomstick over Dymchurch wall". It's best to keep a sharp lookout when driving in this area!

So far you have been circling round the edge of the marsh but now it is time to drive across the middle from west to east. Turn east along the B2067 and 6 miles will bring you to Aldington. This village has been home to a disparate collection of writers.

Make your way first to St. Martin's Church, (TN25 7EG), by turning off the B2067 along Roman Road and then Church Lane. In 1511 the great theologian and scholar **Erasmus (c.1466-1536)** was appointed rector of Aldington, living next to the church in what is now Parsonage Farm. (His predecessor was Thomas Lineacre who became one of Henry VIII's doctors. This village has some impressive connections). Sadly Erasmus did not find his time here very happy. Although he spoke Latin and Dutch, he had very little English and could not communicate very successfully with his congregation – what pearls of wisdom they must have missed. He resigned in 1512 after only one year in the parish, complaining of a kidney complaint, which he blamed on the local beer.

The village has become quite extensive over the years. **Noel Coward (1899-1972)** was the last chairman of the parish of Hurst before its incorporation into the parish of Aldington. He lived at Goldenhurst, a 15th century manor house, on Giggers Green Road (TN25 7BY) between 1929 and 1956. He wrote many songs and lyrics here and it is said that one of them, 'Room with a View', was inspired by the vista from one of the windows. The house was requisitioned during World War II and it was this which caused him to buy White Cliffs in St. Margaret's Bay. Today the house maintains its show biz connections as it is home to novelist and comedian Julian Clary.

'Sign on the entrance to Goldenhurst (now a private house)'

Drive five miles east from here to Postling. This village was home to two writers in the early years of the twentieth century. **Ford Madox Ford (1873-1939)** owned Pent Farm in Stone Street and when the Polish born writer Joseph Conrad needed a home he lived here and wrote 'Lord Jim', 'Typhoon' and 'Nostroma'. He was to have three more homes in the area at Orlestone, Wye and Bishopsbourne and we suggest a visit to the latter if you have more time in this area.

Three miles to the south is Hythe and from here it's a straight forward journey back along the A 259 through Folkestone to Dover.

IF YOU HAVE MORE TIME

A glance at a map will show that the itineraries suggested from Dover almost overlap those we suggest for stays based in Canterbury and Tenterden. A pleasant few hours could be spent exploring some of those bordering areas. In addition, 15 miles from Dover is Bishopsbourne with connections to three very different writers.

The most direct route is north on the A2 (CT4 5HJ). Make your way first to the church. **Richard Hooker (1553-1600)** was rector here for the last five years of his life. He played a significant part in the development of Anglicanism as a middle way between Puritanism and Catholicism writing much of his eight volume seminal book 'Laws of Ecclesiastical Polity' here in Bishopsbourne. There is a memorial to him on the south side of the chancel. Although it is known that he was buried under the chancel floor the exact position is not marked.

The rectory where Hooker lived and wrote his significant book was demolished in 1954, although the old yew hedge is still called Hooker's Hedge. Next door to the church is Oswalds, the late-Georgian successor to Hooker's rectory. This has long been in private hands and was home to the great Polish-born novelist **Joseph Conrad (1857-1924)** from 1920 until his death in 1924. A memorial porch on the village hall was named after him, with contributions largely raised by his American admirers.

'Oswalds'

One more writer made his home in this attractive village (CT4 5HT). Just leave your car parked outside the church and walk for two minutes down The Street, which is immediately in front of you. Look out for Ivy Cottage on your right hand side. **Jocelyn Brook (1908-1966)** spent the last years of his life in this quiet spot and died here in 1966. His major fictional works were 'The Orchid Trilogy' and 'The Dog at Clamberdown' and the plots in both of them are centred in the village. He was also a noted botanist, writing extensively about wildflowers and producing the much sought after standard work on British native orchids. It seems sad that he is not better known today. Look out for the lovely memorial window to him in the cottage, suitably incorporating a wild orchid.

If you are in need for some refreshment now you will find the perfect place straight in front of you. You may feel a selective mermaid cull on the shelves of The Mermaid Inn (CT4 5HX) would be helpful but there is no argument with the warmth of the hosts' welcome or the superb quality of the food. We certainly recommend it.

You are only 4 miles from Canterbury so it would be very easy now to use some of our suggestions for literary exploration in the Canterbury chapter.

Don't forget, though, that there is another potential area to explore. If you have packed your passport it is possible to continue the literary detective work across the channel. A day trip or overnight stay to Calais or Dunkerque is very easily arranged from Dover, since there are frequent sailings to France from the port. In addition, the car ferry through Eurotunnel from Folkestone reaches Calais in just 35 minutes. You could then drive down the A26 to the walled town of Montreuil-sur-Mer, which was **Victor Hugo's (1802-1885)** inspiration for 'Les Miserables'.

Arras is easily accessible from Dunkerque. Situated between the battlefields of Ypres and the Somme there are reminders all around the area of the First World War. It is possible to trace many locations that appear in the work of the First World War Poets. Cambrai is also close by. It was in a forest retreat at nearby Ors that **Wilfred Owen (1893-1918)** wrote his final letter home just one week before the armistice in November 1918.

CAN I DO THESE TOURS WITHOUT A CAR?

If you are a keen cyclist you will find a wealth of National Cycle Routes in the area. The Romney Marsh Meanders are five self-guided rides for both the wobbly novice and the more experienced rider, with routes ranging from 10 to 42 miles. More information is available from the Romney Marsh Countryside Park on 01797 367934 or visit www.rmcp.co.uk for details.

Romney Marsh Countryside Partnership and its sister organization White Cliffs Countryside partnership are also the people to consult for guided walks in the Dover and Folkestone area which will take you close to some of the literary sites we have mentioned. Go to www.whitecliffscountryside.org.uk or telephone 01304 241806 for more information.

BEST TIME TO VISIT

This is an area of literary festivals and the real problem is selecting the most appealing. It might be easier to make several visits!

Every other year (on even years) on August Bank Holiday Monday there is a 'Day of Syn' in Dymchurch which raises money for local charities. Many in the town dress up, there are pageants and re-enactments of encounters between the fictional vicar and the excise men. But be warned! There are usually press gangs patrolling the streets looking for unsuspecting visitors to join His Majesty's Navy. Information is posted on the web site: www.dymchurchdayofsyn.org.uk

It is worth being in Folkestone in the autumn. Every September there is an H.G. Wells Festival celebrating the time when the novelist lived in the town. More information on this is available at www.wellsfestival.com

November sees the annual Folkestone Book Festival when well known writers, critics, radio and TV personalities present a week long programme of discussions, lectures and workshops. Full details of the current programme can be found on folkestonebookfest.com

IF YOU HAVE CHILDREN

Who needs an Adventure Playground when there is a real lighthouse to explore? South Foreland Lighthouse (CT15 6HP) is a lovely Victorian building in St. Margaret's Bay with magnificent views over the English Channel. It's worth the 73 step climb. Find out more information by visiting southforeland@nationaltrust.org.uk or telephone 01304 852463

If you have older, adventurous, children with you they will probably be thrilled to go on the Dover Sea Safari on the 10 metre Rigid Hull Inflatable Boats (RHIB) moored in the Western Docks. There is a variety of trips to choose from-we think the two hour 'Seal Safari' to Pegwell Bay sounds particularly good value. After that adrenalin fuelled trip you should find youngsters quietly grateful for some gentle literary sleuthing. For more information contact Sea Safari on 07870 738580 or email at info@doverseasafari.co.uk

One of the nicest ways to explore Romney Marsh is by the very popular Romney Hythe and Dymchurch Railway. Opened in 1927 it extends for 13.5 miles between Hythe and Dungeness with many of the original locomotives still in operation. Any child in your party (not forgetting the adults' inner child) will love it. Telephone 01797 362353 or visit www.rhdr.org.uk for more information.

And if what you want is an old fashioned, sandcastle building, rock pool exploring environment then youngsters will be blissfully happy in the Folkestone area. The Sunny Sands Beach is within walking distance of Folkestone town centre and west of the town, from Dymchurch round the curve of St. Mary's Bay to Littlestone there are miles of golden sands.

ISLE of THANET

Beside the Seaside at Broadstairs, Margate and Ramsgate

The far north easterly corner of Kent really was an island in its original incarnation and remained so until the sixteenth century. This island was separated from the rest of Kent by the Wantsum Channel but this has gradually silted up and Thanet became part of the mainland. Only the word 'Isle' remains to hint at its independent past. Thanet itself takes its name from the Saxon word 'Tenet', meaning a fire beacon. These were erected along the coast to give warning of an invasion.

The people of Thanet justifiably take great pride in their area and do much to share this with visitors. It is the first destination in Europe to have a Greeter scheme similar to the Big Apple Greeter of New York programme. Thanet Greeters are local volunteers who want to share their enthusiasm for the area with visitors. It's a marvellous free public service. Find out more on www.visitthanet.co.uk or email any questions to info@kentgreeters.co.uk

THANET'S WRITERS

Charles Dickens (1812-1870)

Many writers have come here over the years attracted by the beauty of the region but one name above all others dominates. Kent, especially the Medway towns, was very special to Dickens (have a look at the Rochester chapter where he plays a large role) and Broadstairs in this chapter.

In fact, Dickens said that Broadstairs was his favourite seaside holiday town. He wrote about it with great affection in 'Our English Watering Places' and first spent his summer holidays here in 1836 when, aged only twenty four, he wrote part of 'Pickwick Papers'. After that he returned regularly over the next fourteen years composing 'Nicholas Nickleby', 'The Old Curiosity Shop' and 'Barnaby Rudge' in the town as well as completing 'David Copperfield'. There was a downside to this as his continued patronage made the town very popular. It was no longer the quiet haven he had first discovered and by 1850 he was looking for a different holiday home.

'Dickens' portrait bust on a wall of Bleak House'

Dante Gabriel Rossetti (1828-1882)
Christina Rossetti (1830-1894)

Around the headland from Broadstairs is the small village of Birchington. The poet, painter and founder of the Pre-Raphaelite Brotherhood, Dante Gabriel Rossetti, spent the last months of his life in a bungalow lent to him by the architect.

When he died in 1882, aged 53, he was buried in Birchington churchyard. The memorial cross on his grave was carved by fellow artist Ford Madox Brown and his sister, Christina Rossetti, wrote a memorial poem, 'Birchington Churchyard'. She was already suffering from increasing depression when she came to the funeral with their mother and brother William.

Charles Hamilton, known as Frank Richards, (1876-1961)

Billy Bunter's creator moved to Rose Lawn, a small suburban house in Kingsgate, Broadstairs, in 1926. It remained his home until his death at 86 years old on Christmas Eve 1961. He had never married but had been well looked after by his devoted housekeeper, Miss Edith Hood. She continued living in the house after his death.

Charles Harold St. John Hamilton began his literary career early and had his first children's story accepted almost immediately. After that there was no stopping him. He had found a winning formula, tapping into the universal fascination with boarding school life. With considerable skill he wrote long running stories for a variety of children's magazines such as 'The Gem' and 'The Magnet'. Over the years he went on to create many different schools, each with its distinctive pupils and for each one he adopted a different author pseudonym. It was the long running stories in 'The Magnet' about the greedy, dishonest Billy Bunter of Greyfriars School, who always got his come-uppance, that led to his lasting fame.

'The Magnet' closed in 1940 but the Greyfriars stories were then published in a hardback series in 1947. Later Charles Hamilton (but better known as Frank Richards) wrote the TV scripts for seven series of Billy Bunter stories between 1952 and 1961.

With his various pen names he is believed to have written about 100 million words in his lifetime and featured in the Guinness Book of Records as the world's most prolific writer.

Oliver Postgate (1925-2008)

This animator, puppeteer and writer is probably best known for creations such as Ivor the Engine, Bagpuss and the sublime Clangers, those surreal creatures who dominated children's TV programmes in the 1960s and 1970s. All were made by Smallfilms, the firm set up by Oliver Postgate with his business partner, Peter Firmin, working out of a disused cowshed on the Firmin's farm at Blean outside Canterbury. It was an easy commute for Oliver from Broadstairs.

Although he lived a quiet life here with his family, his genius was recognized by the outside world. In 1987 the University of Kent at Canterbury awarded him an honorary degree. Somewhat to the University's surprise (though perhaps not, they were well aware of his modesty as well as his genius) Postgate announced that the degree was really intended for Bagpuss and subsequently the old saggy cloth cat, baggy and a bit loose at the seams, was displayed in academic dress. Perhaps he was right. After all, in a 1999 poll Bagpuss was voted the most popular children's TV programme of all time.

Oliver Postgate died, aged 83 on 8 December 2008 in a nursing home near his home in Broadstairs. He is remembered with great affection in the town. Local artist, Martin Cheek, was commissioned by Mr.Postgate's partner, Naomi Linnell, to create a fitting mosaic to reflect the animator's personality. As a result it is the Clangers who delightfully appear on the side of his Chandos Square house.

ONE DAY VISIT

The whole of this suggested itinerary is given over to Broadstairs. For information before you arrive go to www.visitthanet.co.uk or telephone 01843 577577. Many places on the tour have associations with Charles Dickens and you'll find plaques marking houses where he stayed and also several shops and businesses featuring a genuine or spurious Dickens link. Look out for The Old Curiosity Shop Tea Rooms, The Barnaby Rudge pub and Nicklebys' Cafe. You get the picture!

Dickens stayed here with his family for at least one month every summer from 1839 until 1851 and these visits helped to develop the town's burgeoning tourist industry. In a letter to a friend, he wrote: "You cannot think how delightful and fresh the place (i.e. Broadstairs) is and how good the walks" and it is very easy to see why. Even in the twenty first century the town still has many visitors. Its unspoilt charm, its sandy beaches and the slower, almost 1950s pace of life are all very attractive. It really is the quintessential seaside town.

Things were not always so quiet and gentle. In 1723 **Daniel Defoe (c.1660-1731)** was here researching information for his mammoth guide 'A Tour through the Whole Island of Great Britain 1724-1727'. He describes the small fishing hamlet of 300 souls "of which 27 follow the occupation of fishing. The rest would seem to have no visible means of support. I am told the area is a hotbed of smuggling. When I asked if this was so, the locals did give me the notion that if I persisted in this line of enquiry serious injury might befall my person".

You should have no such problems in today's exploration. Incidentally, you may be tempted to search out the 'broad stairs' of the town's name. You are doomed to failure as it is actually a corruption of the original Anglo Saxon name 'Bradstow' meaning 'broad place'.

The seaside town's late Victorian popularity has also left a very tempting legacy. Many Italian settlers came here to open ice cream parlours and, in addition to these, there are now two famous 1950s Italian cafes offering the ultimate in handmade ice cream.

All the Dickens' sites are in close proximity to each other. We suggest you park your car, if you have driven here, at Prospect Place car park, which is also close to the railway station. **Charles Dickens** came to the town in 1837, staying in lodgings in the High Street. Aged only 25, he spent the summer finishing off 'The Pickwick Papers' which launched his literary career. Over the next fourteen years he and his family spent many summers here. It was always a full household.

Dickens was very gregarious and the prolific writer was constantly sending invitations to his many friends to join him and his family beside the sea.

Turn right out of the car park into Nelson Place which becomes Harbour Road (it's very nautical around here, as befits an ancient fishing port) and walk towards the arched gateway. On your left, at the entrance to Fort Road, is Archway House which spans the walkway. Dickens knew it by the less precise name of Lawn House.

As you look back you will see a plaque on the archway stating that two novels were completed here: 'The Old Curiosity Shop' (1840) and

'Barnaby Rudge' (1841). Dickens' output was quite phenomenal and he can't have allowed himself much holiday relaxation time. He did, though, have great self discipline and after a morning of work would join the crowds on the beach. He emerged from a bathing machine as "a kind of salmon coloured porpoise-splashing around in the ocean".

'Bleak House'

Make your way up Fort Road to Bleak House (CT10 1EY), the castellated house on the edge of the cliff overlooking the harbour; it dominates the skyline. This was Dickens favourite holiday home from the mid-1840s to 1852 but it's unwise to jump to conclusions too quickly. The novel of the same name is not set in Broadstairs but in Hertfordshire, although some of the initial plotting was certainly done during one of Dickens' annual visits.

Bleak House was then called Fort House, another suitable name for the gaunt mansion. Dickens loved the house and he wrote to the Duke of Devonshire: "In a favourite home of mine perched by itself on top of the cliff with the green corn growing all about it and the larks singing invisible all day long ... the freshness of the sea and the associations of the place - I finished 'David Copperfield' in this same airy nest - have set me to work with great vigour."

Today the house is in private hands and at the time of writing external viewing only is permitted but you should be able to make out Dickens' study, which looks straight out across the sea. On a clear day the French coastline can be seen from this small bay-windowed room. It was here, sometimes working eight hours at a stretch, that he completed the greater part of his personal favourite novel 'David Copperfield'. At least one Broadstairs resident was given a major part in the story. We will find Betsy Trotwood's house later.

The study at Bleak House also appears in **Elizabeth Bowen's (1899-1973)** 1969 novel, 'Eva Trout'. The beginning of the chapter 'A Summer's Day' has a vivid description of the lantern window which hangs out in the air overlooking the sea. In Dickens' day there were also cornfields all around.

By now you may be fully engrossed in tracking down Dickens but there is an interesting diversion to the north along the well sign posted Viking Coastal Trail towards the North Foreland Lighthouse where, one tradition says, the original 39 Steps of **John Buchan's** 1915 novel are situated. Certainly Buchan **(1875-1940)** spent time here in 1914, convalescing from a duodenal ulcer.

When you return to Harbour Road continue walking towards the sea, passing underneath a second archway. As the road veers to the left the Tartar Frigate is on your left. Dickens loved this pub: "the cosiest little sailors' inn that is to be met around the coast". Interestingly, the retired naval officer who loves Rosa Bud in 'The Mystery of Edwin Drood' is Mr.Tartar!

Retrace your steps along Harbour Road to Eldon Place, a small thoroughfare on your left hand side. This leads to Victoria Parade and Dickens House, probably the most interesting site on today's tour. This could, though, be a good moment for lunch, as Dickens House does not normally open until 2.00 pm. As in any seaside town, there is no problem in finding tasty snacks and meals readily available.

Now you are ready to turn into Victoria Parade to visit Dickens House (CT10 1OS). The original Tudor building was much extended in Victorian times with a pretty façade including a wrought iron balcony on the second floor also being added.

This delightful old house has been turned into a fascinating museum to commemorate Dickens' association with Broadstairs. There is also an additional attraction for the Dickens enthusiast. It was once the home (described as " a neat little cottage with cheerful bow window") of Miss Mary Pearson Strong, on whom the writer based much of his character of Miss Betsy Trotwood, David Copperfield's formidable great aunt.

Dickens came to know Miss Strong and watched her fighting a losing battle chasing away the donkey-boys who drove their animals over the green in front of the cottage. He was certainly not going to waste such rich material, although perhaps out of respect for her feelings, the location was moved to Dover.

You will find the curators very informative and helpful but be warned, the museum has limited opening times. It might be worth checking beforehand on 01843 863453 or 01843 861232 or email l.ault@btinternet.com. On the whole it is open for the summer season from Easter, daily between 2.00 pm and 5.00 pm.

When you finally drag yourself away from this fascinating house, turn right for a three minute walk further along Victoria Parade (there's another ice cream parlour along the way). Turn right into Chandos Square and in the far right hand corner is the former home (CT10 1QW) of Oliver Postgate.

After the animator's death, a blue plaque stating very simply that 'Oliver Postgate lived here' was fixed to the house but his partner, Naomi Linnell, also wanted something visual to inform people about his work. The mosaic she subsequently commissioned from local artist Martin Cheek, shows Tiny Clanger and Major Clanger looking up towards the blue plaque on the front wall of the house. Supposedly Tiny Clanger is saying: "Who's Oliver Postgate?" and Major Clanger is replying "You fool he made us".

It took Cheek one month to make this mosaic while the design took him an incredible five minutes only to plan out, with Ms Linnell at his side advising him. It is one of the most stylish memorial plaques we have seen, full of colour and fun. Don't leave Broadstairs without seeing it.

'Oliver Postgate house with Clangers mosaic to the right of the bottom window'

The return journey to the car park is very simple. Retrace your steps to Dickens House then turn left into Albion Street. You will find the Royal Albion Hotel on your right hand side. There is a plaque commemorating Dickens' visit in 1839, (when he wrote some of 'Nicholas Nickleby') although this was actually in the more modest establishment of Ballards Hotel, named after the owner, which occupied the site. Today Ballard is still remembered by the Ballards Lounge at the Royal Albion Hotel. Dickens must have enjoyed that first visit as he returned the following two years and then in 1845 1849 and 1859. On at least one of these visits his fellow writer and good friend, **Wilkie Collins (1824-1889)** stayed with him.

'Royal Albion Hotel'

'Plaque on the wall of the Royal Albion Hotel'

A two minute walk along Albion Street will complete your round trip and bring you back to the car park.

TWO DAY VISIT

If the first day's exploration involved a gentle stroll around Broadstairs, this second day is more easily done by car as you visit other parts of the Isle of Thanet. Distances, however, are not great and the tourist office can provide walking and cycling routes between the major towns. Public transport here is very good too.

We are, however, assuming you are travelling by car so we suggest you first drive north towards Margate. Turn left out of yesterday's Prospect Park car park into Stone Road and join the B2052 to drive north out of Broadstairs. At Joss Bay (CT10 3PG) you will see the North Foreland lighthouse on your left hand side. As a young man **George Bernard Shaw (1856-1950)** applied for the post of lighthouse keeper here. His application was rejected due to his youthful inexperience. One wonders what effect a successful application might have had on his literary career. To the right there is a beautiful sandy beach so you may want to stop to look for the thirty nine steps down to it which, by tradition, are said to have given the title of Buchan's novel.

Continuing along the B2052 you will come to Kingsgate, still part of Broadstairs geographical area. Third on the right is Percy Avenue with The Nineteenth Hole Public House (you are next to the golf course) on the corner. **D.H. Lawrence (1885-1930)** spent a discreet holiday in 1913 at Riley House in Percy Avenue with Frieda Weekley, who was later to become Mrs.Lawrence.

Almost at the end of the avenue, beside the sea, is Rose Lawn (CT10 3LF) Frank Richards' home for 35 years. There is a plaque on the front of the house commemorating the writer's time at this address. Sadly the rose lawns are no more. Today the front garden is laid with more practical paving stones.

Retrace your route along Percy Avenue to George Hill Road and turn right. At the double roundabout take the B2051 to Margate. Queen Elizabeth Avenue becomes Princess Margaret Avenue, signposted Cliftonville Bays. At the miniature golf course turn left onto Palm Bay Avenue which becomes Eastern Esplanade. Look out on the right-hand side between Second and Third Avenues for the Tom Thumb Theatre (CT9 2LB) Information on 01843 221791 or www.tomthumbtheatre. co.uk). The clue is in the name.

This is the smallest theatre in Kent and may be the smallest stage of any public theatre in Great Britain. It measures just 7 feet by 10 feet.

'The Tom Thumb Theatre'

This delightful arts venue was originally built as a coach house in Victorian times and was almost derelict when it was bought by the theatrical agent, Lesley Parr-Byrne in 1984. She and her actress daughter Sarah have lovingly transformed the building into a 58 seat red and gold Victorian style theatre in miniature. It's well worth a visit.

Continue east along the B2052 and join the A255 on the outskirts of Margate. Drive towards the seafront and the Marine Terrace.

Margate is today enjoying a cultural renaissance, especially with the opening of Turner Contemporary (CT9 1HG) telephone 01843 233000. It's on your right hand side as you drive along The Parade but be warned, parking is a nightmare. Turner was a frequent visitor to the town and the new gallery is on the site of the guest house where he stayed.

Opening times are 10.00am to 7.00pm, closed on Mondays. Don't miss the café here. It serves delicious pastries with your coffee and in evenings has an imaginative tapas and full dinner menu. While you are here do make sure you also visit the excellent Tourist Information Office situated behind the gallery. All members of the staff are most helpful and there is a wealth of suggestions on the shelves about spending a most enjoyable time in the area.

After this diversion, continue driving along The Parade and turn left down King Street. Turn left again down Addington Road and you will see the Theatre Royal in front of you (CT9 1PW).

In 1779 a sea captain, Charles Mate, converted a stable into a playhouse. Seven years later, in 1786, he moved his playhouse to the present site with King George III granting it a royal charter – hence the name. It opened to the public in 1787, thus making it the second oldest theatre in Great Britain. One of the first people to perform here was Sarah Siddons and for over a hundred years the theatre enjoyed tremendous popularity. Of course Charles Dickens came here many times from nearby Broadstairs, particularly enjoying "a most excellent performance" of 'As You Like It' in 1847.

George Bernard Shaw arrived here in 1907 to coach a new actor appearing in his play 'John Bull's Other Island'. He was feted as one of the great celebrities of his day. How different from one of his first visits to this area when he failed to secure a job at North Foreland lighthouse.

Later the theatre lost its popularity and became at different times a furniture warehouse, a cinema, a wrestling venue and a bingo hall. What would Captain Mate have thought about that? But today it is once again a very successful theatre (CT9 1PW) or call 01227 787787 for more theatre information.

John Keats (1795-1821) stayed in Margate for a few weeks at a time in 1816 and 1817 while working on 'Endymion'. He found the town "bare and treeless", so surely he must have visited the theatre while he was here.

Starting from the Theatre Royal drive back to Trinity Square. You will see a pretty house, Albion Lodge, with a blue plaque noting it was home to Hattie Jacques and John Le Mesurier during the 1960s. From here turn left at the seafront and drive along Marine Terrace. There is a fascinating literary landmark, the Nayland Rock Shelter, on your right hand side (CT9 1AE). In 1921, while staying at the Albermarle Hotel, in Cliftonville, to recuperate from a nervous breakdown, **T.S. Eliot (1888-1965)** found solace on Margate seafront.

He composed some important lines of 'The Wasteland' as he sat under the roof of this now listed shelter which looks out over the beach. "On Margate Sands/I can connect /nothing with nothing". During his stay at Margate the very bad case of writer's block, which was so depressing him, seems to have been overcome and he was able to complete this pivotal literary work.

'Nayland Rock Shelter'

Margate has a long standing reputation as a popular seaside resort. It can claim two important seaside firsts: beach donkey rides in 1780 and deckchairs in 1898 both started here. Probably your backseat passengers may be loathe to leave, but there are still many literary treasures waiting to be discovered in Thanet.

Our next stop is three and a half miles away at Birchington. Drive westward out of Margate along the A28, passing through Westgate-on-Sea, a fashionable seaside resort in Victorian times. In the 1930s **John Betjeman (1906-1984)** stayed in nearby Birchington and wrote:

"Hark I hear the bells of Westgate,
I will tell you what they sigh
Where those minarets and steeples
Prick the open Thanet sky".

As you drive into Birchington you will see All Saints Church straight in front of you (CT7 9RS). To park it is easiest to turn left by the church then right into Kent Gardens and park in the church grounds. The church building dates back to 1350. Close by the porch to the south door of the church is a large Celtic cross, carved by artist **Ford Madox Brown (1821-1893)**. This marks the grave of **Dante Gabriel Rossetti** who was buried here in 1882, after spending the last few months of his life in the village. Although some lettering has now become worn, the grave itself is very well maintained with a mass of glorious bright blooms on the day of our visit. The Rossetti Society is to be commended for its efforts. Inside the church there is a Pre Raphaelite memorial window to the poet. Close by Birchington-on-Sea Railway Station are the Rossetti Memorial Gardens, a very pleasant spot to refresh yourself before continuing on the literary trail.

'Grave of Dante Gabriel Rossetti

The next port of call is inland. From the church turn back a few yards onto the A28 then turn right down Park Lane (helpfully signposted Acol). Drive past Quex Park (CT7 0BH), a Victorian country house with beautiful gardens and vast play areas for children. Now drive one and a half miles south along the B2048 to Acol (pronounced Acole), one of the smallest communities in Kent. It is said to be haunted by the ghost of the infamous Smuggler Bill.

The village's unusual name comes from Old English, meaning Oak Wood. Two writers have immortalised this village in their work. The first was **R.H. Barham (1788-1845)** who was a regular summer visitor to Margate, staying in a house now known as Ingoldsby House. He featured the nearby chalk pit in the story 'The Smuggler's Leap' in his 1840 'Ingoldsby Legends'. He based this gory tale on the local tradition that a riding officer called Anthony Gill was killed here in pursuit of the aforementioned Smuggler Bill. In a thick fog both men went over the precipice and the local legend has it that the place has been haunted ever since.

Between 1908 and 1909 Acol's second famous literary inhabitant, **Baroness Orczy (1865-1947)** (of 'Scarlet Pimpernel' fame) leased Cleve Court, an impressive mansion two miles beyond Acol village on the Minster Road at Monkton (CT12 4BA). She and her husband, the painter Montague Barstow, imported horses from her home in Hungary and drove a carriage with the horses three abreast.

That must have caused some comment among the locals! While living here she finished 'Beau Brocade' and wrote 'Nest of the Sparrowhawk' which is set in Acol.

Continuing today's round trip, drive east along the A253 and follow this road all the way to Ramsgate. You are following in very distinguished foot steps. **Queen Victoria (1819-1901)**, as Princess Victoria, spent many childhood holidays here. In her reminiscences she wrote: "To Ramsgate we used to go frequently in the summer and I remember living in Townley House near the town and going there by steamer".

Frank Muir (1920-1998), the writer and TV personality, was born in Ramsgate and wrote about it in his autobiography 'A Kentish Lad'. Surprisingly for him, he got the title wrong. Those born east of the river Medway are Men of Kent and those born west of the river are Kentish Men.

On the outskirts of Ramsgate take the B2054 to the seafront. The Royal Esplanade becomes St. Augustine's Road. Turn left into Spencer Square, rather reminiscent of the Regency terraces in Bath. Look out for the blue plaque on No. 11 where **Vincent van Gogh (1853-1890)** lodged in 1876 whilst teaching at a language school. How fortunate for art lovers that he gave up the day job. In a letter to his brother, Theo, in the autumn of 1876 he wrote: "If there should be no human being that you can love enough, love the town in which you dwell. I love Paris and London, though I am a child of the pinewoods and the beach in Ramsgate".

We were delighted to see a touching homage to him – on the day of our visit there was a large vase of sunflowers in the sitting room window. One side of the square is the continuation of Royal Road and a plaque outside No.6 marks the language school where van Gogh taught in 1876. There is still a good number of language schools in Thanet.

Go back to St Augustine's Road and veer right to the sea front. The next port of call is Nelson Crescent on the left hand side. Look out for No. 14 (CT11 9JF). Britain's first true detective novelist, **Wilkie Collins (1824-1889)** stayed here on holiday in 1861, but he also had other addresses in Ramsgate, as we shall find on our tour. He spent many holidays here.

Returning to The Royal Parade turn left then right onto Albion Place. Look out for No. 14 (CT11 8HQ). **Jane Austen (1775-1817)** stayed here in 1803 while visiting her brother Frank, a captain in the Channel Fleet, who was charged with fortifying sea defences against Napoleon's expected invasion from France. His sister then used the town at least twice in her novels making it the setting for Wickham's attempted elopement with Darcy's sister in 'Pride and Prejudice' and then for a visit by Tom Bertram in 'Mansfield Park'.

Continue round the square and turn left at the top into Wellington Crescent. The famous poet and philosopher, **Samuel Taylor Coleridge (1772-1834)** came here frequently in the summer months from 1816. There is a blue plaque outside No.3, his favourite lodgings (CT11 8JL). His health was not robust and he became an enthusiastic sea bather believing this would be beneficial. Describing his favourite view he wrote:

> "Dismounting from my steed I'll stray
> Beneath the cliffs of Dumpton Bay,
> Where Ramsgate and Broadstairs between
> Rude caves and gated doors are seen."

Wilkie Collins also stayed in Wellington Crescent during visits in the 1830s.

Ramsgate certainly welcomed a variety of visitors in Victorian times. One name may perhaps be somewhat unexpected. From Wellington Crescent turn left up Augusta Road then right at the end into Bellevue Road then left into Artillery Road. There is a blue plaque outside No. 6 (CT11 8PU) marking the home of **Jenny Marx (1814-1881)**, eldest daughter of the more famous Karl.

The founder of Marxism stayed here with his beloved daughter in 1880. The simple terraced house seems so appropriate for one who identified as closely as he did with the working class. In all **Karl Marx** came nine times to Ramsgate at other times staying nearby at No. 62 in the magnificently titled Plains of Waterloo, part of your route back via Wellington Crescent to the seafront.

You will see the Oak Hotel (CT11 8LN) on Harbour Parade. Charles Dickens visited Ramsgate frequently on his way to Broadstairs, making the six hour journey from London by paddle steamer. He would then stay overnight at the Royal Oak Hotel. In 1847 his friend **Hans Christian Anderson (1805-1875)** left the hotel to return to Denmark after his first English tour. He wrote that Dickens: "had walked from Broadstairs to say good bye to me and was in a green Scotch dress and gaily coloured shirt ... He was the last person to shake my hand in England."

R.M. Ballantyne (1825-1894) knew that sea very well too. The author of 'Coral Island' stayed here in Ramsgate researching for his stories 'The Lifeboat' (1864) and 'The Floating Light of the Goodwin Sands' (1870) and was able to persuade the coxswain, Isaac Jarman, to let him sail the tug accompanying the lifeboat.

You'll probably agree you've managed to fit in a very full and varied day in the footsteps of a wide variety of writers. You may want to linger longer in Ramsgate but if not the A235 will take you back to Broadstairs, from where you started.

CAN I DO THESE TOURS WITHOUT A CAR?

Yes you can.

If you are a cyclist you will be thrilled to find the 27 mile Viking Coastal Trail, one of the most attractive leisure cycle routes in Kent. As it runs along the coast it's a good starting point to explore most of the sites described in this chapter. To find out more about this family friendly cycling go to www.visitthanet.co.uk or contact Visitor Information Services on 01843 577 577.

The local Tourist Board has done so much to encourage visitor interest in the area. Imaginatively it has created the Turner and Dickens Walk, connecting Margate and Broadstairs, so recognizing the two towns' links with the great writer and great painter. The gentle walk is only four miles long. One of the nicest features is the mosaic panels installed in each town. Broadstairs mosaic artist Martin Cheek (who created the memorial plaque to Oliver Postgate) worked with children from two schools close to the walk to create the mosaics. Go to www. turnerandickenswalk.co.uk or call Thanet Tourist Information on 0870 264 6111for more information.

If by now your feet are killing you, (and we all know that feeling!) consult Stagecoach for information on local bus services.

Telephone 0871 2002233 or go to www.stagecoachbus.com

BEST TIME TO VISIT

Broadstairs returns Dickens' affection by holding an annual Dickens Festival every June This tradition started in 1937 to commemorate the centenary of Dickens first visit and except during World War II has been held every year since. It began as a three day event, then six days and now lasts an amazing eight days. The streets are filled with people in Dickensian costumes and many of his characters are brought to life. Full information is at www.broadstairsdickensfestival.co.uk

IF YOU HAVE CHILDREN

This area really is child heaven with fifteen sandy beaches, a number of which hold the coveted European Blue Flag award. These include all the seaside towns mentioned in this chapter. There is everything you need in the area for a traditional seaside holiday with sandcastles, funfairs and ice cream whilst the more athletic will love the opportunities for surfing, jet skiing and kite surfing. More information can be found in 'Our Beaches are Beautiful' from Visitor Information Centres or downloaded from www.visitthanet.co.uk

On the Ramsgate Road outside Margate is the Hornby Visitor Centre (CT9 4JX) where you can see and interact with what are probably some of Britain's favourite toys such as Scalextric, Airfix and Corgi. The youngsters will really enjoy it but we suspect it's the 'Big Kids' who will most love the trip down Memory Lane. (James May made a TV documentary about it.)

It's normally open Wednesday to Sunday but go to www.hornby.com/visitorscentre or call 018943 233524 for more information.

As you drive south from Birchington you will pass Quex Park (CT7 0BH). It is well worth stopping at this Victorian Country House with its fascinating private museum filled with objects and animals from Africa and Asia. There's a huge indoor soft play, beautiful gardens, a Falconry Centre and in summer a Maize Maze to get lost in. All the information you need is on www.quexpark.co.uk or call 01843 842168.

MAIDSTONE

A Day in the County Town

Maidstone is appropriately situated in the middle of the county. One's first impression is of a modern administrative centre criss-crossed by busy roads, but there is still some feel of the old town in the area around the historic Archbishop's Palace and the parish church. Several statesmen and politicians have left their mark here. Some even claim **Wat Tyler (1341-1381)**, the leader of the 1381 Peasants Revolt, came from Maidstone, but so little is known of him that this is impossible to verify.

In All Saints Church (once described as "the grandest perpendicular church in England") there is a memorial to George Washington's family who originated from Maidstone before they emigrated to America. Their Coat of Arms can be seen there. Incredibly, it seems to foretell the future importance of the family to the United States as it contains stars and stripes. In 1837, the statesman and novelist, **Benjamin Disraeli (1804-1881)** became the town's MP (he of the wonderful comment on the publication of 'Daniel Deronda': "When I want to read a novel I write one!"). The Maidstone M.P. became Prime Minister, but the demands of high office did not prevent him producing novels such as his most famous trilogy 'Coningsby' in 1844, 'Sybil' in 1845 and 'Tancred' in 1847 right up to 'Endymion' in 1880. Those were much more leisured times.

It would be difficult for a twenty first century Prime Minister to find the time to produce such a literary body of work. In the late twentieth century, however, **Ann Widdecombe (1947-)**, the town's devoted M.P. for 23 years, also turned her many talents to writing. She published her first, very readable, novel, 'The Clematis Tree' in 2000. It became a best seller and three other novels have been published with a promise of more to follow.

MAIDSTONE'S WRITERS

Sir Thomas Wyatt (1503-1542)

Sir Thomas Wyatt, one of the 'silver poets' of the sixteenth century, shares with the Earl of Surrey the credit for introducing the sonnet form into English poetry. It seems quite amazing that there was time for such literary innovation when so much else was happening in his short but eventful life.

This poet and diplomat was born and brought up fewer than four miles from the centre of Maidstone, at Allington Castle. At only 17 years old he was married to Elizabeth, daughter of Lord Cobham, but it seems likely that the great love of his life was Anne Boleyn from nearby Hever Castle. Certainly a jealous Henry VIII thought so and Wyatt was imprisoned in the Tower of London. From his prison window he may have witnessed the execution of his presumed mistress.

Wyatt was luckier. He was released unharmed, possibly through the good offices of Thomas Cromwell, although there was to be a second brief period of imprisonment four years later. Wyatt was only 39 when he died unexpectedly of a fever. Conspiracy theorists at court were of course quick to whisper how convenient his death was as the king was thought to be interested in making Elizabeth, Wyatt's widow, his wife and his sixth queen. But that dubious honour was ultimately reserved for Catherine Parr.

What a headstrong family the Wyatts were. The poet's son, also called Sir Thomas Wyatt, joined the ill planned conspiracy against Queen Mary which came to bear his name. Unfortunately for him he seems to have had far fewer influential friends than his father at court and he was executed in 1554.

"Noli me tangere for Caesar's I am", wrote Wyatt in a clear poetical references to his affair with Anne Boleyn. In fact, neither this poem nor any of his others was read widely in his lifetime. All were first printed fifteen years after his death in 'Tottel's Miscellany' of 1557.

William Hazlitt (1778-1830)

It is sad that perhaps the greatest essayist and critic in the English Language is so little known today. Much of his work is now out of print and some of his most pertinent comments are in danger of being lost for ever. There is a timeless wisdom about "He who undervalues himself is justly undervalued by others", "The love of liberty is the love of others, the love of power is the love of ourselves" and "When anything ceases to be a subject of controversy it ceases to be a subject of interest."

The author of these epigrams, and a wealth of other writing, was born in Mitre Street, Maidstone on the 10th of April 1778 but had left the town by the time he was two. His father was a Unitarian minister and the family became used to a peripatetic lifestyle as the Rev'd. William Hazlitt (the critic son was confusingly named after his father) was moved from one church to another. Three years after their stay in Maidstone, they were in America where William senior preached, lectured and founded the First Unitarian Church in Boston. Fortunately for the literary detective, Maidstone recognizes its eminent literary son in the Hazlitt Theatre and the Hazlitt Arts Centre.

Edward Thomas (1878-1917)

The poet and critic was only 23 when, accompanied by his wife Helen and their son Merfyn, he moved to the picturesque village of Bearsted, on the eastern outskirts of Maidstone. They were to spend three years here in two different cottages. The first one, Rose Acre (Thomas described it as "damp and ugly" with no roses until he planted them), was a mile from the village at the foot of the North Downs. It is no longer there. The family subsequently moved to Ivy Cottage, now Ivy House, which can still be seen on The Green.

'Ivy House with wall plaque for Edward Thomas

While living in Bearsted, Thomas published two volumes of essays: 'Horae Solitariae' (1902) and 'Rose Acre Papers' (1904), as well as some reviews but no poetry. In fact it was not until the outbreak of the First World War, when he was 36 and encouraged by Robert Frost, that he started to write the poetry which was to give him his later fame. His poetic output was crammed into three full years. He was killed at Arras in 1917 before his first collection was published.

In spite of his strong Welsh roots, both his parents being Welsh, Thomas clearly had great affection for Kent. In 1904 he left Bearsted with his wife and two children (a daughter Bronwen had been born while they were there) and for the next two years they lived in Sevenoaks Weald (see the Sevenoaks chapter for more information).

ONE DAY VISIT

When planning your visit you might find it helpful to download The Maidstone Official Visitor Guide iPhone App, available from the App Store. This gives access to an interactive guide of what's on, where to stay and what to do in and around Maidstone.

All the literary sites are conveniently close together in the centre of town and easily accessible from Maidstone East railway station or from Fremlin Walk Car Park (ME14 1PS). From the railway station walk down Station Road to St. Faith's Street. The north exit from the car park will also bring you to St. Faith's Street and Maidstone Museum, housed in an Elizabethan manor house (ME14 1LH), telephone 01622 602838.

The museum does possess **William Hazlitt's** writing desk and death mask but at present these are kept safely under lock and key in the archives. Also recently housed in the same building is the Tourist Information Centre. The staff there are very helpful and will answer all your questions.

'Maidstone Museum'

You now need to be at the south exit from the car park. If it's not too busy the simplest way is to use the car park as a short cut and go straight through. Immediately in front of you on Earl Street is the Hazlitt Theatre.

'Hazlitt Theatre'

Turn left and two minutes walk will bring you to the intersection of Earl Street and Rose Yard. Hazlitt was born here but the house, close to his father's Unitarian Chapel in Bullock Lane, has since disappeared (ME14 1HP). Turn right down Rose Yard. This narrow winding alley is very atmospheric and it is easy to picture what it would have looked like two hundred years ago in Hazlitt's time. You will pass Hazlitt Arts Centre on your right hand side (ME14 1PL), which offers a varied programme of drama and music as well as a traditional Christmas pantomime. Telephone 016222 758611 for more details. At the end of the alley you will come out into the High Street.

Turn right, walking past the Town Hall, a lovely Georgian building dating from 1762, then left into Mill Street and next to the medieval Archbishop's Palace you will see All Saints Church in front of you (ME15 6YE).

It is well worth a visit. **Laurence Washington**, great uncle of **George Washington (1732-1799)**, lived in a mansion (sadly no longer there) in the magnificently named Knightrider Street and is buried in the churchyard of All Saints. Inside the church is the memorial to George Washington's family. The church (free admission but donations welcome) is open Tuesday to Thursday between Easter and September from 10.00am to 4.00pm and

Saturdays from 10.00am to 12.30pm. Much more information is available at www.visitmaidstone.com or call 01622 843298

It is an easy matter to return to Fremlins car park. Either retrace your steps or go straight ahead along Fairmeadow when you get to the High Street.

The rest of today's literary detective work involves a drive around the outskirts of the town. This area richly deserves its title of 'The Garden of England'. Traditionally Londoners came here picking hops, the only chance poor children were likely to have to breathe good country air and certainly their only chance of a holiday whilst their parents were hard at work. In 1931 **George Orwell (1903-1950)** (Eric Blair's *nom de plume*) spent 18 days hop picking in the area as he attempted to identify with those at the very bottom of society. He had previously been sleeping in a London doss house and two tramps he had met there accompanied him to Kent.

Once in the Maidstone area they lived in a hopper hut made of corrugated iron - not the romantic environment the Old Etonian had imagined - and earned nine shillings a week each. Orwell observed that a family of gypsies, much more skilled at the work than him, having picked hops every year since birth, were able to earn fourteen shillings a week each.

There is some debate where Orwell's hop farm was. It was possibly Home Farm in Wateringbury (now a built up area of offices and housing) or possibly Blest's Farm in West Malling. Orwell wrote about the experience in the essay 'Hop Picking' and also used the experience in his 1935 novel 'A Clergyman's Daughter'.

You may feel it's worthwhile to drive west out of Maidstone to soak up some of the atmosphere where Orwell may have been hop picking.

But if time is limited we suggest you head in the opposite direction to Bearsted, three miles east of Maidstone. As in many busy towns, Maidstone operates a well sign-posted one way traffic system in the town centre. Follow the signs along the A249 to Ashford from the High Street along Wat Tyler Way, which becomes King Street and then Ashford Road (A20). You enter Bearsted in an area of recent development and this picturesque village has become almost a residential suburb for Maidstone. Turn left along pretty Yeoman's Lane to reach the village green.

This area round The Green with its half-timbered houses, gourmet pubs and restaurants has been home to three very different writers.

'Bearsted Village Green and pond'

In 1901 the 23 year old **Edward Thomas** moved here with his wife Helen and son Merfyn. They were to spend three years in the village before moving to Sevenoaks Weald. Their first cottage has disappeared over time but they later moved to Ivy Cottage (now called Ivy House). It's almost opposite the White Horse Inn, overlooking the North side of the Green and just across the road from the pond.

If you look closely you will see an attractive simple stone memorial on the outside of the house stating 'Edward Thomas Poet and Writer Lived here'. Next door is a house called Wheelwrights. Not surprisingly it was the wheelwright's shop in Thomas's day. ME14 4DV will get you there.

Continue along The Street, turning right beside the Green and almost diametrically opposite to Ivy House, in Church Lane, is Bell House (ME14 4ED). The American novelist, **Sinclair Lewis (1885-1951)**, spent two months in Bearsted in the summer of 1921. He was busy writing 'Babbitt' to be published the following year. His short stay finished at the end of September when he left this perfect example of an English village for the cosmopolitan charms of Paris.

'Bell House'

Turn right into Yeoman's Lane on the fourth side of The Green. When you first came into the village you drove past Snowfield (ME14 4DH), a magnificent house set back from the road behind high gates. **Baroness Orczy,** of 'Scarlet Pimpernel' fame, lived here with her husband, the artist Montague Barstow, after moving to the village from Acol near Ramsgate (see Isle of Thanet chapter for more information on this earlier period of her life). This was one of their three homes; they also had a large London home and a grand villa in Monte Carlo.

It was often said that when she was in residence in Bearsted, Baroness Orczy would see herself as the Lady of the Manor, always travelling in a coach and four and demanding respect. She was furious if village girls did not curtsey or village boys omitted to doff their caps when she passed. She must have forgiven the village's negligence, as she saw it, since Snowfield remained one of her favourite homes until her death in 1947.

It is difficult to see past the entrance gates to the house but you may be amused to note that a small, recently built, estate of nearby houses has entered into the spirit of its former illustrious neighbour. As you seek him here and seek him there you'll find both Pimpernel Close and Blakeney Close.

You may be tempted to continue south east along The Street, joining the A20 to visit lovely Leeds Castle. That's probably the game plan of the young backseat passengers, especially if they have heard of its Go Ape attraction.

To continue the literary trail, however, we suggest you drive north of Maidstone to the pretty village of Boxley, off the M20 at junction 6. The simplest way there from Bearsted is back via the A249. Boxley parish includes several hamlets including Boxley itself and Sandling. In spite of being only 4 miles from the centre of Maidstone and close to the motorway, the area is surrounded by woodland and certainly maintains a very 'villagey' feel.

Alfred Lord Tennyson (1809-1892) often stayed with his younger sister, Cecelia, at Park House in Sandling. The description of the summer fete which opens his 1847 poem 'The Princess' is believed to be based on one held at Park House five years earlier. Sandling is also traditionally believed to be the original for Dingley Dell in Charles Dickens' 'Pickwick Papers'.

'Boxley Church'

Boxley Church (ME14 3DR) is well worth a visit, parts of it date back to the thirteenth century. The churchyard is kept as unspoilt as possible and it provides a peaceful haven with its wild flowers and butterflies. In fact it is difficult to believe one is so close to a busy motorway. Surely little has changed immediately around the church since Cecelia Tennyson's wedding to **Edmund Lushington (1811-1893)**.

When he wrote 'In Memoriam' in 1850 after the death of his great friend Arthur Hallam, Tennyson described his sister's wedding here:

"O happy hour, behold the bride
With him to whom her hand I gave
They leave the porch, they pass the grave
That has today its sunny side."

Earlier in the poem he shares fond memories of: "maidens of the place/That pelt us in the porch with flowers".

Inside Boxley Church Tennyson's name appears on his sister's memorial in the south aisle. Also in the church look out for the memorial above the choir stalls on the north wall of the chancel to **Sir Francis Wiat (1588-1644)** (the earlier spelling of Wyatt). This governor of Virginia from 1621 is buried here. The memorial traces his family tree back to Henry Wiat, father of Thomas Wyatt, the poet. A strong rebellious strain ran through the family. An ancestor, Henry Wyatt, fell foul of king Richard III, and was imprisoned in the Tower of London. Tradition has it that a stray cat adopted him, snuggling up to give him warmth and then devotedly bringing him a (dead) pigeon a day for dinner. Fortunately Wyatt was able to persuade his gaoler to cook these 'presents' for him. Colloquially the cat has become known as 'The Caterer Cat', for obvious reasons.

Also in Sandling is Kent Life, formerly The Museum of Kent Life (ME14 3AU), an award winning open air museum with a collection of historic buildings showing life in Kent over the past 150 years. You could easily spend all day here but if time is short head for Ma Larkins' Kitchen based on H.E. Bates' novels and the "perfick" world of Kentish villages around Ashford and Little Chart, where he lived for 40 years. The exhibit has been hidden away on this site for the past few years but the original set is now being faithfully restored. Telephone 01622 763936 or visit www.kentlife.org for more information.

'Kent Life'

This probably marks the end of a full day's exploration but there are further suggestions included below either for this day or to be done later.

IF YOU HAVE MORE TIME

Nine miles south of Maidstone is an interesting, if sombre, area with close connections with Charles Dickens. On Friday, the 9th of June 1865, the novelist was returning from a stay in France with the actress **Ellen Ternan (1839-1914)** and her mother when their train from Folkestone was involved in a very serious crash. The timetable for the Boat Train varied, according to the tides, and on this fateful day it was misread by the workmen repairing a gap in the railway line across the River Beult, a tributary of the River Medway between Staplehurst and Headcorn. They erroneously believed they had two clear hours for emergency repairs.

Instead the train jumped the gap and eight of its coaches crashed down the river bank, killing 10 passengers and seriously injuring 49. Dickens and his companions were in the first carriage which remained coupled to the brake van.

Apart from cuts and bruises they were not injured. Ellen and her mother were quickly removed from the scene and then Dickens played a major part in helping the injured and dying. Three hours after the crash, when he had done all he could for the casualties, he crawled back into his carriage - a very risky manoeuvre - to rescue the latest instalment of 'Our Mutual Friend' which he had been proof reading at the time of the crash.

He seems to have been remarkably calm and collected at the time but he was later to suffer from what today would be called Post Traumatic Stress. In 1868 wrote: "My escape in the Staplehurst accident of three years ago is not obliterated from my nervous system. To this hour I have vague rushes of terror, even when riding in a hansom cab, which are perfectly unreasonable but quite insurmountable".

There is one curious footnote to this dreadful incident. Dickens died at his beloved Kent home, Gadshill, on the 9th of June 1870, five years to the day after the Staplehurst disaster.

The journey to the site of this tragedy is straight forward. Take the A229 due south from Maidstone town centre. This road has a number of local names including Week Street and both Lower then Upper Stone Street. As it becomes Loose Street, Barton Road is on the left. This is the site of Maidstone Grammar School (ME15 7BT). The school has a long and distinguished history. Some traditions suggest the poet **Christopher Smart (1722-1771)** was a pupil here. What, however, is not in doubt is that Nobel Prize winning author **William Golding (1911-1993)** taught English and Music at the school between 1938 and 1940 and also met his future wife here. Perhaps Piggy, Ralph, Jack and the other schoolboys in his 1954 novel 'Lord of the Flies' had real life originals in Maidstone.

Continue along the A229 to Staplehurst, the route being clearly marked.

CAN I DO THESE TOURS WITHOUT A CAR?

As in all major towns it is perfectly possible and often much easier, to get around unhindered by the need to find a parking place. There are two mainline train stations in Maidstone and National Rail Enquiries on 08457 484950 can give you all the information you need. There is also a railway station at Bearsted.

'River boat'

Leaving the urban area, the nicest way to reach Sandling and Boxley is by river boat. Kentish Lady sails between Easter and October from moorings by the Archbishop's Palace in the town centre. Call 01622 753 740 for more information. The No.155 bus from Maidstone stops at Kent Life.

BEST TIME TO VISIT

Although every season has its own attractions it is worth remembering that The Heart of Kent where Maidstone lies is not known as The Garden of England for nothing and many visitors look forward especially to the apple blossom in the Spring.

This area is famous too for its hop gardens where the hops used for making beer are trained up long poles until they are ready for harvesting in the autumn. Every September you can join in the fun at the hop picking festival at the Beer, Hop Picking and Music Weekend at Kent Life (ME14 3AU).

IF YOU HAVE CHILDREN

You will need to time your visit to Kent Life very carefully if you have children with you as once there they will be so caught up in the various attractions there are sure to be tears before bed if you try to hurry them away. It's a marvellous site, catering for all members of the family with its historic buildings, Adventure Playground and Farmyard (not forgetting Ma Larkins' Kitchen). Find out more information on www. kentlife.org.uk or call 01622 763936

It is easy to combine your detective work into the three writers at Bearsted with a visit to Leeds Castle (ME17 1PL). Surrounded by 500 acres of parkland and set on two islands in the middle of a lake, it has been described as the loveliest castle in England. It was the favourite country retreat of Edward I's queen, Eleanor of Castile and of Catherine de Valois, widow of Henry V. Its last private owner, Lady Olive Baillie, gave it to the nation in 1976. While you are enjoying the beauty, youngsters can let off steam in the Knights Realm Playground. For the really adventurous there is 'Go Ape', a high wire forest adventure course high above the tree tops with rope bridges and Tarzan swings. More information for both the castle and playground can be found on www.leeds-castle.com/atak or by calling 01622 765400

ROCHESTER

Medway's Dazzling Dickensian Delights

Rochester, together with Chatham, Gillingham, Rainham and Strood make up Medway, which takes its name from the river that flows through it. The area is quite a literary rarity, as instead of associations with several writers it is dominated by just one – Charles Dickens. So this chapter deals almost exclusively with the great novelist, though you will find some reference to other writers in the itineraries. In the main they are mentioned here because they came to Rochester to visit their friend Dickens.

Charles Dickens (1812-1870)

Dickens' life was a tale of two cities - London and Rochester and the one he saw as the ultimate source of happiness was Rochester. The area between the rivers Medway and Thames was the scene of his happiest childhood memories. His father, a kind hearted, generous man, utterly incapable of living within his means, was a clerk at the Navy Pay Office. Almost certainly Mr.Micawber is an affectionate portrait of him.

In 1817, when Charles was five, his father was posted to Chatham Dockyard. The Dickens family were to live in Chatham for five happy years. In his free time John took his young son exploring the surrounding countryside, sometimes passing Gads Hill Place, situated on a hill top overlooking Rochester. Built little more than thirty years previously, in 1780, for a former mayor of the town, the red brick Queen Anne house was still comparatively new.

In later life Dickens wrote that it seemed to him as a child "the most beautiful house ever seen". His father told him that if he worked very hard he might one day be able to afford to buy it. Probably neither of them actually believed then that it would happen, but fate plays strange tricks.

'Gads Hill Place, Higham'

The family (Charles was the second of eight children, two dying in infancy) became used to frequent changes of address. Sometimes this was because of John Dickens' job. The family homes form a catalogue of major naval ports: Portsmouth, London, and Chatham. But sometimes there was a grimmer reason to move - to escape the ever present creditors caused by John Dickens' over lavish lifestyle. In 1824, when Charles was twelve, matters came to a head. The family by then was living in London. His father was arrested and confined in the Marshalsea Debtors' Prison. To help the family finances, twelve year old Charles had been sent to work in the sordid conditions of Warren's Blacking Factory. His childhood was abruptly over.

At this bleakest moment, like Mr Micawber's frequently expressed hope, something did turn up. Charles' maternal grandmother died and John Dickens' £450 inheritance paid off the debts and life gradually returned to relative normality. There was even sufficient money for Charles to be educated at Wellington House Academy for the next two and a half years. It is easy to see, however, how Dickens must have yearned for his carefree childhood in Kent and how his father's words about Gads Hill Place must have stuck in his mind.

Twelve years later, Dickens, now twenty four, was starting to make something of a literary name for himself. His day job was newspaper reporting but in the evenings he was writing fiction. 'Sketches by Boz' had been published to enthusiastic reviews and he was immediately commissioned to write 20 monthly instalments of what was to become 'The Pickwick Papers'. He felt in a sufficiently sound financial position (always that worry about money - surely a hangover from his childhood traumas) to marry. On the 2nd of April 1836 he married Catherine Hogarth, the daughter of his publisher. And where did they spend their honeymoon? In the village of Chalk, little more than a mile from his dream home of Gads Hill.

'Lesleys Cottage, the Dickens' honeymoon retreat'

Fast forward 20 years and 10 children and by 1856 the marriage had irreparably broken down. Charles Dickens was rich and famous. He had written ten major novels, many short stories (including 'A Christmas Carol') and edited the popular weekly 'Household Words' but it is not always easy to be the wife of the public's darling. Catherine suffered from depression and drank heavily; she had grown fat and unattractive. It seemed that separate households would be a good solution to the couple's misery.

In 1857 Dickens issued a formal statement declaring that his wife "suffered from a mental disorder" that made her unfit to be his wife and that she had "never cared for their children nor they for her".

Incredibly, it was as the marriage was disintegrating that Gads Hill Place, with all its memories of a joyful childhood, came on the market. He bought it for £1,790 (it was the only house he ever owned rather than rented). His original plan was to use it as a summer residence and to let it in winter but after his formal separation from Catherine in 1858 it became his permanent home until his death in 1870. John Dickens had died in 1851. How proud he would have been that his son was now so successful he was the owner of the house of his dreams.

Charles was not alone at Gads Hill. His sister in law, Georgina Hogarth, had lived with the Dickens' family since she was 15 to help her sister bring up the children. (In fact in the early days of their marriage it was another sister, Mary, who had performed the same role. Tragically, to Dickens' great distress, Mary died in his arms, aged just 17. He wore her ring on his little finger for the rest of his life). Georgina supported her brother in law on the marriage break-up and continued to live in his household. Quite a shocking decision in Victorian England. Only Charlie, the eldest child, stayed with his mother after the separation.

There was, however, quite possibly, one other long term and significant visitor to Gads Hill Place. The final straw for Dickens' unhappy marriage was probably in 1857, when he fell in love with the 18 year old actress Ellen Ternan. He succeeded in keeping this relationship secret from his adoring public but he did buy her homes in England and France and it seems likely she bore him a son who died in infancy.

ONE DAY VISIT

Dickens loved Rochester and the city loved him. It loves him still. Everywhere you go you will be reminded of the great writer and his characters, especially those who populate 'Great Expectations' and 'The Mystery of Edwin Drood'. Both of these were written when he lived outside Rochester at Gads Hill Place. There are fifteen buildings still standing which feature in various novels. When you pause for refreshments the name of the café or shop is likely to remind you of them. Peggotty's Parlour in the High Street and Tiny Tim's Tearooms (01634 06615) at the entrance to the Cathedral car park are two of our favourites.

There are convenient car parks close to the High Street at Blue Boar Lane, Boley Hill and the Cathedral. If you arrive by train, come out of the station and turn right into the High Street. Go straight ahead keeping the Cathedral tower clearly in view. It dominates the landscape and makes an effective landmark.

The Visitor Information Centre at 94 High Street makes a good starting point. Contact the helpful people here on www.visitmedway. org or telephone 01634 338141 for lots of useful information about the area. It also has a very pleasant café. From here a circular tour will take in most of the major Dickens sites. All are signposted. It may take three hours at a gentle ramble but much depends, of course, on how long is spent at various attractions.

Immediately next door to the Tourist Office is The Six Poor Travellers' House, founded by Richard Watts, MP for Rochester in 1563 and 1571, as an overnight lodging house for honest wayfarers or tramps to receive a night's free bed and board. Remember Richard Watts' name - we shall be meeting him again later on this trip.

Dickens visited the house in 1854 and used it later that year in the Christmas story 'The Seven Poor Travellers', describing the "clean white house of a staid and venerable air, with a queer old door". Today it is a fascinating museum open between March and October (at the time of writing closed on Monday and Tuesday) with free admission, although donations are welcome. Both the house and its beautiful courtyard herb garden are well worth a visit.

'The Six Poor Travellers House'

The next Dickensian site, Eastgate House, is three minutes walk away on the same side of the road. In Dickens' time this was a girls' school and as such appears as a seminary for young ladies in 'The Mystery of Edwin Drood' and as Westgate House girls' boarding school in 'The Pickwick Papers'. Until recently it was used as The Dickens Centre. It has now been scheduled for restoration and conversion into an arts centre and gallery.

'Swiss Chalet'

Do make a point of going into the garden behind the house where you will see an original Swiss chalet, Dickens' stylish study, relocated here from Gads Hill Place.

It was sent in 98 numbered sections, in 58 packing cases, from Switzerland by his actor friend Charles Fechter in 1864. If you have ever struggled to make up bookcases and cupboards from flat packs, spare a moment's sympathy for the great writer. Before he could have a private retreat for writing, all the pieces had to be fitted together. The gigantic puzzle must have been put together successfully, since he then used the chalet as his summer study for the next six years.

The upper room became his favourite writing spot and he installed mirrors to reflect the light, writing to a friend "My room is up among the branches of the trees; the birds and butterflies fly in and out". He wrote his last words in this upper room in the garden of Gads Hill before his death on the 9th of June 1870. Today the chalet is beginning to show its age and is supported inside by steel props to secure the structure. An appeal has been launched for its restoration (for details see www. dickensfellowship.org).

Also in the garden, on the left as you leave, is the restored horse-powered well pump installed by Dickens at Gads Hill Place in 1857. It was moved here in 1973 to ensure its preservation.

Return to the front of Eastgate House and on the other side of the road, almost opposite, is a handsome half timbered building. This was originally one large house but by Dickens' time it had been divided up into three separate dwellings. In 'Great Expectations' it was Mr.Pumblechook's home where he carried out his business as a corn chandler. Dickens then used it again in 'The Mystery of Edwin Drood' where it became the home of Mr.Sapsea, the mayor of Cloisterham.

'Uncle Pumblechook's house with wall plaque'

Turn right back to the High Street and then left into Crow Lane and make your way up the hill. On the left is the imposing Restoration House (so called because Charles II is believed to have stayed here on his way to London in 1660 when the monarchy was restored). This is the original of Miss Havisham's Satis House - but this one is still standing and has not been consumed by fire. There is a story that three days before his death, Dickens was seen leaning on the opposite wall staring long and hard at the house. Perhaps he intended recycling this building in his work as he had done with many other Rochester properties. At the time of writing it is open to visitors between June and September on Thursdays and Fridays from 10.00am until 5.00pm (more information on 01634 848520 or www.restorationhouse.co.uk).

'Restoration House with a plaque on its wall'

There are steps opposite the house. Go up these and continue through The Vines. This was originally the priory vineyard of Rochester Cathedral and was called The Monks' Vineyard in 'Edwin Drood'. In Victorian times it had become a meadow so it is easy to imagine the apprehensive young Pip making his way through here to visit Miss Havisham in her big house. Ten years after Dickens' death "the nooks and ruins where the monks had once had their refectories and gardens" were laid out as a public park. Don't miss the superb modern sculpture of a monk near the wall at the far end of the park. This more than life-size work has been carved from a single tree trunk.

Take the right hand path and go through the gap in the wall. Keep going, you are nearly at the cathedral. Turn right then immediately left into Minor Canon Row. This was built in 1723 to accommodate the Cathedral canons and organist. In 'The Mystery of Edwin Drood' this was Minor Canon Corner. It still possesses the same gentle appeal that Dickens described. **Dame Sybil Thorndike (1882-1976)**, the renowned actress, and her novelist brother, **Russell Thorndike (1885-1972)**, lived here as their father was a canon of the cathedral. In fact Dame Sybil later claimed that her earliest acting experience was performing plays in the Castle Gardens.

Now the route turns right, cutting through King's School, founded in 1542, although there is a tradition that an earlier school was founded here at the same time as the cathedral. A short distance will bring you to an iron gate, called Prior's Gate, with steps going downwards.

Go via these into the Cathedral. It dates from A.D.604 and is the second oldest in the country. Much of the plot of 'Edwin Drood' is set here. The Dean and Chapter have placed a brass memorial to Dickens in the middle of the wall in the South Transept, the first turn on your left hand side after entering through Prior's Gate.

Walk through the cathedral with its beautiful Norman architecture in the nave and crypt (and on a more practical level the tea rooms are excellent). Come out through the main West Door and cross the road. You are now beneath the majestic walls of Rochester Castle. In Dickens' time the castle moat was part of the graveyard of St. Nicholas church, next door to the cathedral and Dickens had wanted to be buried there quietly.

His adoring public had much grander plans for him and The Times newspaper's suggestion that he should be buried in Westminster Abbey was immediately adopted.

You will see a number of gravestones against a wall. Alongside is a small tablet set in the wall detailing this, although it omits the popular belief that Dickens' ghost is said to haunt the castle moat. Incidentally, there never was any water in the moat, it was more a defensive ditch and until 1960 there were houses there.

'Plaque indicating where Dickens wished to be buried'

Turn left and follow the road round to Baker's Walk and go through the columns decorated by the heads of stone lions. You will now see a cream coloured house in the corner with a very familiar name. This is Satis House (ME1 1TE), once the home of Richard Watts, the founder of Six Poor Travellers' House. When Elizabeth I stayed here in 1573 she was less than enthusiastic about her entertainment. It was satis – enough. And the name has stuck. It would be difficult to imagine this pretty house, almost completely rebuilt in the eighteenth century, being the model for Miss Havisham's gloomy abode but it certainly furnished its ironic name. Today it is the administrative centre for King's School.

'Satis House'

Retrace your steps to the cathedral with Rochester Castle on your left hand side. "Magnificent ruin!" said Mr.Snodgrass. "Glorious Pile!" echoed Mr.Jingle as the members of The Pickwick Club travelled over Rochester Bridge and saw the castle for the first time. If you have the time it is well worth exploring the castle more fully. The keep is one of the best preserved examples of Norman architecture in England.

Between the cathedral and St. Nicholas church is a small graveyard. The fourth headstone to the left of the cathedral wall is a memorial to the Dorrett family which may have been Dickens' inspiration for the central characters' names in 'Little Dorrit'. Certainly he is believed to have wandered in local graveyards looking for suitable names for his characters.

'Dorrett memorial'

Carry on down Boley Hill and pass through Jasper's Gatehouse. Chertseys, a 15th century house, is next door and Chertsey's Gate is inside the arch set into the wall. In 'The Mystery of Edwin Drood' these two buildings are described as if they were one, linked together by a connecting door with Edwin Drood's wicked uncle, John Jasper, the cathedral choir master, inhabiting the rooms above the gatehouse and Mr Tope the chief verger living next door. Had the novel been finished who knows what dark deeds might have taken place here. So much of Rochester is in the novel and the final words Dickens wrote were about the "very neat clean breakfast that Mrs Tope laid out for their lodger".

Next door is Topes restaurant, the home of Mr.Tope, the Chief Verger. It is the last building mentioned in the writings of Charles Dickens.

'Topes Restaurant'

You are now almost back where you started from in the High Street but there are still three more buildings to see.

Turn left and almost immediately in front of you is The Old Corn Exchange with its enormous clock which has a cameo role in 'The Uncommercial Traveller'. You can't miss the "queer old clock which projects over the pavement".

'Old clock'

Next door on the left is The Guildhall where Pip was formally apprenticed to "dear, good, noble, Joe Gargery" in 'Great Expectations'. You may want to spend some time here as the museum has two excellent galleries dedicated to Charles Dickens and his life and works including a recreation of the Prison Hulks - the kind of ship from which Magwitch escaped. Across the hallway is a small audio visual theatre showing a short film on Dickens. It was made on location in and around Rochester and among other gems is a rare chance to see inside the Dickens' Chalet, now closed to the public while repairs are made. More information is available on 01643 848717 or at www.visitmedway.org

On the opposite side of the High Street is the Royal Victoria and Bull Hotel. The Royal was added in 1836 after Princess - later Queen - Victoria's stay. It is still very much in business as a hotel. Meetings of The Pickwick Club took place here and in a sense still do every June in re-enactments during the Dickens Festival. The hotel also features in 'Great Expectations' as The Blue Boar.

And now you have completed the circular tour and are back where you started. The suggested morning tour probably takes about three hours but you may want to adopt a more leisurely pace and spread the sightseeing over several days.

If you are ready to continue your explorations after lunch you will be travelling by car to the village of Cooling north of Rochester (ME3 8DG) to get you to the churchyard and 'Pip's Graves'. Take the A2 out of Rochester, then the A228 to High Halstow and Grain and follow the signs to Cooling. The atmospheric opening scene of 'Great Expectations', written in 1860 when Dickens was living at nearby Gads Hill Place, is set here. Just over one hundred years earlier in 1770 the Kentish historian, Edward Hasted, wrote: "Cooling is an unfrequented place, the roads of which are deep and miry." What a lonely place this part of the Hoo Peninsula must have been then. Even today the small scattered village feels cut off in spite of the distant view of oil refineries and terminals two miles away in the Thames Estuary.

They are much more recent of course. All Pip saw were bleak marshes.

The thirteenth century church of St. James, Cooling (ME3 8DG) is on the edge of Cooling Marshes, the road bending twice to go round the churchyard. If it's a grey winter afternoon when you are visiting it's very easy to imagine the desperate criminal Magwitch hiding behind the gravestones. Gads Hill Place is just over five miles away and Dickens would often take friends from there across the fields to Cooling churchyard to show them the unusual tombstones; "the strange little stone lozenges" of various sizes marking thirteen children's graves from just two families. All the children died in infancy. In Dickens' imagination this site became the final resting place of Pip's little brothers.

'13 children's gravestones'

The winding lane next passes the ruins of Cooling Castle (ME3 8DT) with its magnificent gateway dating from about 1385. The castle was once home to Sir John Oldcastle who died in 1385. The play 'The First Part of Sir John Oldcastle' was included in the 3rd and 4th Folios but scholars do not now believe it was written by Shakespeare. He certainly did write 'Henry IV Part 1' with its depiction of Prince Hal and Falstaff's attempted robbery at Gads Hill but that scene of crime visit must wait for the Day Two exploration.

After this lonely isolated spot you may be ready to retrace your route to Rochester's brighter lights ready for Day Two.

TWO DAY VISIT

If Day One visit was in search of Dickens' fictional characters, then Day Two is mainly in pursuit of Dickens himself, first in his boyhood home of Chatham and then in the area around his beloved final home of Gads Hill Place. He was not the only literary figure who spent time here. In 1784 the young **William Cobbett (1763-1835)** came to the town.

It was to be some time before he made his reputation as a journalist and political writer. Instead he wanted to see the world and enlisted as a foot soldier on sixpence a day in the 54th Regiment of Foot. He spent much of his free time the following year educating himself in grammar, which earned him an extra two pence a day as a corporal before he sailed with his regiment from Gravesend for Halifax in Nova Scotia.

He had fond memories of the area and in his magnificent 'Rural Rides' of 1830 he wrote: "One thing I will say for young women of these towns (Rochester and Chatham) is that I always found those of them that I had the greatest happiness to be acquainted with, evince a sincere desire to do their best to smooth the inequalities of life and to give us 'brave fellows' as often as they could strong beer when their churlish masters or fathers or husbands would have drenched us to death with small." As so often, one feels that the whole story is not being told.

Although Dickens spent those five happy boyhood years here in Chatham there is very little concrete evidence left to show for it. The town looks very different from the one he knew. Before the coming of the railway there was still quite a country feel to the area around the port and the adult Dickens remembered the long country walks he took with his father with great nostalgia. Today a vast regeneration scheme has been in operation in Chatham. This is a workaday town which still has some very attractive Victorian architecture off the beaten path but it doesn't have the instant appeal for the tourist of nearby Rochester. The dockyard, where John Dickens worked and which supported the Royal Navy for 400 years, has now been transformed into a major visitor attraction.

If you arrive in Chatham by train you will be well placed for the first Dickens landmark. As you come out of the station turn left and you are virtually next door to his childhood home in Ordnance Terrace at right angles to the station. In 1817, the five year old Dickens and his parents moved into No.2, now No.11 (ME4 6PT) and stayed there for four years.

There's a simple plaque marking Dickens' boyhood home. The syntax is unusual: "In this house Charles Dickens lived 1817-1821". The three storey terrace houses are modest but there are attractive touches. Each one has a flight of steps with a fanlight over the individual front doors.

If the exterior of the houses has changed little, the surrounding area looks very different today. Rail travel had yet to be invented in 1817 and there was farmland behind the house and fields in front. In 'The Uncommercial Traveller', written in 1860 at Gads Hill, Dickens describes arriving at the railway station which had taken over the "departed glories" of the fields where he played games in his youth. Even at that idyllic time, however, there was a hint of John Dickens' future financial woes. In 1821, to save money, the family down sized to a smaller house in The Brook. It has since been demolished.

'No.11 Ordnance Terrace with its plaque'

You might, however, be travelling by car from Rochester as the two towns run into one another. Make your way to Chatham High Street. You will need to park the car as a large part of the town centre is pedestrianised. Turn right down Railway Street and a five minute walk will bring you to the train station with Ordnance Terrace beside it (ME4 6PT).

Retrace your steps to the High Street and the next turning on the right hand side is Clover Street with some very useful information about the young Dickens on a Tourist Information Board. He attended Mr.William Giles' Clover Lane Academy in 1821-1822 in this street. As the information board states: "Under Mr.Giles' tutelage Dickens would have learned advanced reading, writing, calculating and possibly Latin."

Near here the young Dickens had his first taste of performing to a live audience at the Mitre Inn and the next door Clarence Hotel. His father would stand him on a stool or table where he would sing songs and recite short stories learnt by heart. There would be plenty of tips for him afterwards and a hot dinner. The Mitre Inn became immortalised as 'The Holly Tree' in 'The Christmas Stories' but both it and the Clarence Hotel have now disappeared through redevelopment and the shell of the building has been transformed into the Trafalgar Centre.

Although very few buildings remain in Chatham that have a direct connection with the Dickens family, the town does have a spectacular indoor visitor complex based around his life, books and times and you may feel the best use of time is to spend a morning here. You will probably need about three hours to do it justice. Appropriately Dickens World is at the historic dockyard close by where John Dickens worked. If you have found it difficult to imagine what Chatham looked like in 1817, you will be delighted to find that the sights, sounds and smells of the nineteenth century have been recreated here.

Dickens loved the theatre and he would surely have loved this attraction. To whet your appetite there's a boat ride through Dickensian London, Dotheboys – a Victorian schoolroom and Peggotty's Boathouse. Porters, a pleasant restaurant, is next door and there are plenty of other eating places in the Historic Dockyard area.

For more information call 01634 890421 or www.dickensworld. co.uk. The easiest way to reach all this is either by car (ME4 4LL) or the Medway Mainline bus: 140/141 hop on hop off service, running every 10 minutes.

There is a nice sense of symmetry if you follow your morning visit to Dickens' boyhood home of Chatham by an afternoon visit to his final home of Gads Hill Place in the small village of Higham, about three miles north west of Rochester. The house became a school in 1924 and today it is a co-educational day school.

Go to www.gadshill.org or call 01474 822366 for information about opening times to the general public. If however you just want a sense of place, the outside of the school is clearly visible from the road.

Drive out of Chatham through Rochester crossing the bridge. Take the A226 following signs to Gravesend.

Dickens bought Gads Hill Place in 1856 for £1,790 from **Eliza Lynn (1822-1898)**, later known as the novelist **(Mrs.) Eliza Lynn Linton,** even though there was one major disadvantage to the property. The main road runs through it but it would have taken more than this inconvenience to deter Dickens from buying his dream home. Instead he took a practical approach and had a tunnel dug to link the garden and the shrubbery. It was in this shrubbery that he put the Swiss chalet which became his study where he wrote 'Great Expectations', 'The Uncommercial Traveller', 'Our Mutual Friend' and the unfinished 'Edwin Drood'. He made other structural changes, restoring the conservatory and putting a false bookcase on the inside of the study door. The tunnel still remains today.

The property had been so imprinted in Dickens' mind from those childhood walks with his father that it had already appeared in at least one of his stories. In 'The Christmas Carol' of 1843 it becomes Scrooge's old school. 'The Ghost of Christmas Past' leads the old miser to "a mansion of dull red brick with a little weathercock-surmounted cupola on the roof and a bell hanging in it". This guidebook complements and simplifies what you can learn from Dickens' original novels.

Life was not all writing and Dickens entertained lavishly in the fourteen years he lived at Gads Hill. The railways were criss-crossing England now and many famous fellow authors alighted over the years from the London train at Higham Station about a mile from his home. **Hans Christian Anderson (1805-1875)** was invited for two weeks (but stayed for five!) and Dickens' great friend **Wilkie Collins (1824-1889)**, widely regarded as the inventor of the English detective story, visited very often. In 1860 Katey Dickens, the novelist's second daughter, married Charles Collins, Wilkie's artist brother, in Higham Church (ME3 7LS), a mile north of the village, on the edge of the Thames marshes.

The bridegroom was a semi invalid, twelve years older than the twenty year old bride. It doesn't seem to have been a love match, at least not on Katey's part. She left for her honeymoon wearing black - surely not a good omen. It was however an excuse for elaborate celebrations with a special train bringing guests from London to Higham station. Only one important guest was missing. Catherine, the bride's mother, was not invited. Ten years after these celebrations, Higham Station saw the beginning of Dickens' final journey as his body was taken to London before the very simple funeral in Westminster Abbey.

One of the attractions for Dickens of moving to Gads Hill Place, apart from fulfilling his boyhood dream, was that Shakespeare had immortalised the area in 'Henry IV Part 1'. At one time the hamlet was notorious for the highway robbers who congregated here to attack travellers on the old Dover road. Horses pulling heavy carriages had to be slowed down to walking pace to negotiate the steep hill and passengers were then an easy prey to ambush. This potentially terrifying ordeal was given a slapstick treatment in Shakespeare's play when Falstaff and his cronies' robbery plans were spectacularly unsuccessful – not that the fat knight had any intention of admitting that.

Dick Turpin, the fictional character in the 1834 novel 'Rookwood' by **Harrison Ainsworth (1805-1882)**, was probably based on the highwayman 'Swift' Nick Nevison who operated around here. He deserved his nickname.

Tradition has it that he robbed a man at 4.00am one summer day in 1676 on this stretch of road and then allegedly caught the ferry to Essex and rode furiously to York. He was able to show himself at the bowling green at 8.00pm the same evening and so was able to give himself an alibi which secured his acquittal. Dangerous journeys along here continued and **Daniel Defoe (c.1660-1731)**, in his mammoth volume 'A Tour through the Whole Island of Great Britain' of 1724-1727, wrote that "the place was noted for robbers of seamen after they have received their pay at Chatham".

Today's danger comes from the speed of passing traffic so take care as you cross the A226, which runs past Gads Hill Place. The Sir John Falstaff Inn (Tel 01634 717104) is a short distance away on the opposite side of the road. Dickens would often go across the road for a drink there, or had beer sent over to his house. The obliging landlord acted as a banker to the novelist and regularly cashed his cheques. With its Dickensian wall etchings the inn still makes a pleasant place for refreshment.

'Sir John Falstaff pub'

There is one more village close by with Dickensian connections. Continue driving along the A226 to Chalk, on the outskirts of Gravesend. Chalk church, which is mentioned in the Doomsday Book, still stands overlooking the marshes. In April 1836 Charles Dickens brought his new bride, Catherine, on honeymoon to what was then a remote marshland area but although it is well documented that the couple were here in Chalk village, where exactly they stayed is another matter. Two houses close to each other on the Lower Higham Road both claim that honour.

The imposing Manor House is on the left hand side, on the corner of Vicarage Lane, as you enter Chalk from Gads Hill. Lesleys Cottage (once known as Craddock's Cottage and almost universally now referred to as Honeymoon Cottage) is about 100 yards further down the road on the opposite side.

This pretty weatherboard building has a bust of Dickens over the front door and a plaque stating that this is where he spent his honeymoon. The debate continues as to which cottage was the honeymoon destination but, interestingly, Dickens was drafting 'Pickwick Papers' while he and Catherine were in Chalk and Mr Pickwick stayed with a certain Mrs Craddock while he was on his way to Bath.

As you drive out of the village towards Gravesend on the Lower Higham Road look out on the left hand side for the recently renovated 16th century building which is generally believed to be the original for Joe Gargery's workshop. The forge leads straight into the kitchen. The weather boarded structure is now a private house. Dickens would have seen it on his frequent walks from nearby Gads Hill Place but in 1860 when he wrote 'Great Expectations' there were several other similar forges in the area and it is difficult to have complete certainty which one was Dickens' inspiration.

'The Forge'

Continue along the A 226, to Gravesend. Joseph Conrad spent much of his life in Kent and is buried in Canterbury. His 1902 powerful novella 'The Heart of Darkness' is set in the Belgian Congo but it is told by the narrator, Marlow, to a group of men aboard a ship lying off Gravesend. If you can spare the time from literary sleuthing do go to St.George's churchyard in Gravesend where the North American princess, **Pocahontas (1595-1617)** lies buried 3000 miles from her native land. She died sailing down the Thames on her way back to Virginia, having spent several months in England with her husband, Captain Rolfe.

A short drive further along the A226 brings you to Dartford on the Kent/London border. To break the journey to her brother's house at Godmersham Park, **Jane Austen (1775-1817)** stayed here twice at the Bull and George (now a chemist shop) in the High Street. As she wrote to her sister, she and her mother shared a room "up two pairs of stairs" as they wanted "a sitt. g room and chambers on the same floor". On st visit t¹ d a supper of beef steaks and a boiled fowl but as "no oyster sauce".

way back to Rochester is to retrace your route along the A 226 but it is easy to make a diversion to Cobham along the B2009. Dickens knew this village when he was a boy and mentions it in 'The Pickwick Papers' and he also used to walk here from Gads Hill Place when he lived here. You will certainly get a sense of place by driving through but we suggest a longer visit will do it more justice (see below).

IF YOU HAVE MORE TIME

Take the A2 out of Rochester to Cobham, four miles west of Rochester. The turning off to Cobham Hall (DA12 3BL) is clearly signposted.

Young Dickens and his father used to walk out here on their country hikes and one of the adult Dickens' favourite walks when he lived at Gads Hill Place was through Cobham Park. The owner, Lord Darnley, considerately gave him a key to let himself in. Dickens had earlier imagined Mr Pickwick and his companions walking this way.

"They emerged upon an open park with an ancient hall, displaying the quaint and picturesque architecture of Elizabeth's time". This is Cobham Hall, now a leading girls' boarding school and so very rarely open to visitors. You could try enquiries@cobhamhall.com or call 01444 823371 to see if any public openings are imminent but for an insight into how it looked in Victorian times have a look at its description in 'The Uncommercial Traveller'.

Turn left out of the end of Cobham Hall drive and take the first exit (turning left) at the next roundabout. This is Halfpence Lane to Cobham. Bear right onto The Street.

On your right hand side is the Leather Bottle Inn (DA12 3BZ) built in 1629 and now become something of a shrine to Dickens' life and work, although part of it was damaged by fire in the 1880s. The walls are covered with nearly 1400 photographs and drawings and in the hotel reception area is the chair in which Dickens allegedly sat whenever he visited the inn. The inn was the setting for a number of incidents in 'The Pickwick Papers' (1837). (Note: if you visit opening time is 11.00am)

'Leather Bottle Inn'

Opposite the Leather Bottle Inn is Cobham Church. Dickens describes it in 'The Pickwick Papers' as: "one of the most peaceful and secluded churchyards in Kent where the wild flowers mingle with the grass and the soft landscape around forms the fairest spot in the garden of England". It was one of the places he himself suggested for his burial but this quiet spot, like the graveyard beside Rochester Castle, was turned down in its turn by those in power who arranged his funeral. Nowhere but Westminster Abbey was good enough for the great writer. Perhaps, though, as you leave this peaceful oasis for the bustle of urban life in Medway, it may not be too fanciful to imagine his spirit here in the area that meant so much to him.

CAN I DO THESE TOURS WITHOUT A CAR?

The short answer to this is "very easily". The mainline railway stations at Rochester and Chatham have frequent services from London Victoria and Charing Cross (information at www.southeasternrailway.co.uk and travel from Europe is equally straightforward with Ebbsfleet International station only 20 minutes by coach from Medway. Visit www.eurostar.com for details.

Rochester and Chatham Historic Dockyard are linked by Arriva's Medway Mainline Service 140/141. It's a convenient hop on and hop off service covering places of interest on its route. Visit www. medwaymainline.co.uk for more information.

The Heron Trail, part of the Sustrans National Cycle network, is a circular route covering 18 miles (29kms) which should take about two hours to cycle. Among others it links the villages of Higham, Cooling and Hoo.

Medway Council have this and many other detailed cycle and tourist maps available at the Visitor Information Centre or by emailing transport.planning@medway.gov.uk

Clearly the only way to explore Rochester is on foot. Of course we hope that all you need to know is included in this guide but feel we ought to mention as well the Footsteps in Time guided tour. Go to www.footstepsintimerochester.co.uk or telephone 01634 818630. It's more than a walking tour as some of Dickens most famous characters, including Nancy (called "the tart with a heart" in the tours publicity) provide information and entertainment around Rochester

BEST TIME TO VISIT

It is very tempting to talk about the best of times and the worst of times where Dickens is concerned. Much depends on what you are looking for as you follow this particular writer. You may want to avoid crowds and potter round out of season but it is worth noting that Rochester has built up an enviable reputation for its spectacular Dickens Festivals in June and December with street entertainment, readings and parades. For much more information visit www.whatsonmedway.co.org or call 01634 338141.

IF YOU HAVE CHILDREN

The whole family should have a superb time at Dickens' World, next door to the Historic Dockyard (also well worth a visit) in Chatham. We have suggested a morning here on the itinerary for Day Two. In addition to experiencing the sights, sounds, and smells of Victorian England, there is also the chance to work off some excess energy in the wonderfully titled Fagin's Den, a soft play area for younger children. For more information visit www.dickensworld.co.uk or call 01634 848717.

If you are a dedicated shopper try to negotiate some time off while the rest of the party supervise the youngsters in Fagin's Den. We recommend Dockside Factory Outlet, with its discounted stores selling famous leading brands.

If the children are insisting that all this talk of Dickens is too much like school, take them to Diggerland (ME2 2NU) at Medway Valley Leisure Park in Strood. It's just off J2 of the M2. It advertises itself as the ultimate adventure park experience offering children and adults alike the chance to drive real diggers. Call 0871 2277007 or visit www.diggerland.com for more information.

And if you feel that a park should have some connection with trees, water and wildlife consider a visit to Capstone Farm Country Park in Gillingham. This lovely country park has been awarded the Green Flag national standard. The No. 155 bus from Chatham Rail Station runs hourly in this direction. Much more information is available on www.medway.gov.uk or call 01634 338192.

ROYAL TUNBRIDGE WELLS

Spa Treatments

———➤•◄———

Over four hundred years ago, in 1606, a young aristocrat, Dudley, Lord North, riding between Eridge and Tonbridge discovered the Chalybeate Spring. As he told his friends how rejuvenated he felt from drinking the iron rich water, he could surely not have foreseen how significant this claim was to be. For more than two hundred years the tiny settlement, conveniently close to London, became increasingly popular as news of the health giving waters spread.

One of the first fashionable visitors was Queen Henrietta Maria (the wife of King Charles I). She must have been anxious to take the waters, for in 1629 this "hamlet in the parish of Speldhurst" was nowhere near ready for the tourist trade. She had to camp on the Common as there was no other lodging available.

Visitors from London flocked here, however, and by Georgian times the spa town had gained a reputation as one of the most fashionable places to see and be seen. The legacy of this historic past can be seen in the beautiful Regency architecture of the town. Surprisingly, the 'Royal' prefix does not date from the town's eighteenth century glory days, but from the visit of King Edward VII in 1909.

'Chalybeate Spring and its wall plaque'

TUNBRIDGE WELLS' WRITERS

Daniel Defoe (c1660-1731)

The journalist and novelist is, probably, most famous for being the author of 'Robinson Crusoe', the first English novel. In fact he wrote over 250 works including 'A Tour through the Whole Island of Great Britain, 1724-1727', in which Tunbridge Wells makes one of its earliest literary appearances. He arrived at the most opportune moment as the Prince of Wales was visiting, so there were even more people than usual in the town.

"The ladies that appear here are indeed the glory of the place: the coming to the Wells to drink the water is a mere matter of custom: some drink, more do not. But company and diversion is in short the main business of the place and those people who have nothing to do anywhere else seem to be the only people who have anything to do at Tunbridge. In a word Tunbridge wants nothing that can add to the felicities of life or that can make a man or woman completely happy, always provided they have money; for without money a man is no-body at Tunbridge".

Ironically the reason Defoe had to hurry away from the town was because he himself was "without money". Perhaps there is a coded message about this in his comments about the town.

Fanny Burney (Madame d'Arblay) (1752-1849)

Nearly two hundred years after the Chalybeate Spring was first discovered, Tunbridge Wells still had its fashionable reputation and Fanny stayed in 1778, soon after the publication of her novel 'Evelina'.

She was, however, seriously underwhelmed by the town's charms. She wrote about her visit in her 'Letters and Diaries', published in 1846. "The Sussex Hotel where we lived is situated at the side of The Pantiles, or public walk, so called because paved with pantiles; it has no beauty of itself, and borrows none from foreign aid as it has only common houses at one side and little millinery and Tunbridge–ware shops at the other, and each end is choked up by building that intercept all prospect. How such a place could first be made a fashionable pleasure-walk, everybody must wonder."

'Pantiles Hotel (formerly the Royal Victoria Hotel)'

There could be a very human explanation for this jaundiced view. The dramatist, **Richard Cumberland (1732-1811)**, caricatured by

Sheridan in 'The Critic' as Sir Fretful Plagiary (one gets the picture!), had settled in the town. Fanny Burney, in her diaries, mentions the airs his wife and daughters assumed, even though Cumberland's plays had lost their popularity and were no longer performed. She had been warned that the curmudgeonly playwright hated successful authors and would not want to speak to her. This was to be the case and must inevitably have marred her visit.

Her time here was not wasted, however, as she set some scenes in her 1796 novel 'Camilla' on the town's Mount Ephraim

William Makepeace Thackeray (1811-1863)

In the same year that Cumberland died, the author of 'Vanity Fair' was born in Calcutta, where his father worked for the East India Company. A new age in literature was dawning. Thackeray spent part of his childhood in the spa town, staying with his parents in a cottage on the Common. As editor of the Cornhill Magazine and a distinguished novelist, he returned to spend the last three years of his life here in another house on the Common, today fittingly named Thackeray House.

Here he wrote a good deal of 'The Virginians', which is set in Tunbridge Wells.

He also published a short piece called 'Tunbridge Toys'. In the latter, he gives a vivid description of himself as a fourteen year old borrowing books from the "well remembered library on the Pantiles" and returning to "a dark room in a little house hard by on the Common". His parents were away in London for two days and he was on his own with only a "grim old maid servant" to look after him.

As he sat at night in the lonely drawing room poring over the Gothic novel 'Manfroni or the One Handed Monk' he was too frightened to move and "scarcely dared to turn round". What a shame it is now out of print. It would be fascinating to read what it was that stirred the boy's imagination.

'Thackeray House (now a restaurant) with a wall plaque'

Siegfried Sassoon (1886-1967)

Five miles north east of Tunbridge Wells, on the B2160, is the village of Matfield with its ornate neo-Gothic house, Weirleigh. Siegfried Sassoon's parents had bought the house in 1884 after it was advertised in The Times and in September 1886 it was the birthplace of Siegfried, the second of three boys.

Inside the tall red brick house, however, there was to be great unhappiness. Alfred Sassoon, a Jewish merchant trader, had been cut off by his family for marrying outside the faith. He left his wife, Theresa, when the children were still very young and died not long afterwards. The loss of his father was to be a major influence on Sassoon's development.

In spite of that, so much of his poetry, most especially 'The Old Century', is full of nostalgic memories of time spent in the countryside around Matfield, in what seems to have been a truly idyllic country childhood. He didn't go to school until he was fourteen. In late Victorian England life could be very comfortable for the middle classes and, even though Siegfried was excluded from the Sassoon fortune, he did have a private income which meant he had no worries about supporting himself. And it was at Weirleigh that he arranged for his first poems to be published.

Weirleigh remained the family home until the death of Siegfried's mother in 1947.

'Weirleigh'

Tonbridge School and its literary Old Boys.

The famous five hundred year old school at Tonbridge, five miles from Royal Tunbridge Wells, numbers many distinguished literary figures among its Old Boys. In its publicity the school states that it wishes to foster a life-long empathy for the needs and views of others by adopting as its motto the words of the great novelist and Old Tonbridgean, E.M.Forster: "only connect". An inspiring thought.

Apart from **Edward Morgan Forster (1879-1970)**, the school's roll call also includes World War Two poet **Sidney Keyes (1922-1943)**, novelist and poet **Vikram Seth (1952-)**, novelist **Frederick Forsyth (1938-)** and bookshop founder **Tim Waterstone (1939-)**.

With similar ages, the school careers of the last two overlapped and surely that was not the only time their paths would have crossed.

ONE DAY VISIT

A special heritage Walking Trail through Royal Tunbridge Wells was inaugurated in 2006 to celebrate the 400th anniversary of the discovery of the Chalybeate Spring. The town's excellent Tourist Information Centre can supply attractive self-guiding leaflets for this and answer all your other questions. We suggest you contact them before your arrival on 01892 515675 or see the website www.visittunbridgewells.com The Tourist Information Centre is in the Old Fish Market in The Pantiles (TN2 5TN) and makes an excellent first port of call.

There is good parking in the vicinity but, if you want to leave the car at home, The Pantiles is only a five minute walk from the railway station. The walk around the town itself should take about two hours, leaving plenty of time for a nice lunch before tackling the afternoon literary trail which will take you out of the town to Tonbridge. Of course, in keeping with the spirit of the place, you need to stroll in an elegant promenade. Twenty first century rush would certainly be considered vulgar by the ghosts of the past.

The Pantiles area is where all the action was in the town's fashionable heyday. Even today this traffic free shopping area keeps the spirit of an earlier more leisurely age. It is a paved walkway, shaded by trees and sometimes called The Walks or The Promenade. You may be lucky and catch musicians serenading promenaders from the 'Musick Gallery' above No.43 and in summer time there are frequent open air concerts.

Guided Walking Tours of The Pantiles are held every Thursday and Saturday morning between March and December, starting at 11.30am. It's an excellent way to learn more about Tunbridge Wells and its visitors. Tickets and details are available from the Tourist Information Office.

At the southern end of the Pantiles is the Corn Exchange, originally a theatre built in 1801. Its later incarnation is marked by the carving of the Goddess of the Harvest still visible on the top of the building. Today, in its third life, the building is full of shops and a café but the claret coloured Heritage Plaque to **Edmund Kean (1789-1833)** is a reminder that one of the greatest Shakespearian actors of his day performed at this small theatre.

'The Corn Exchange with a wall plaque to the right of the entrance'

On the opposite side is The Royal Victoria and Sussex Hotel, also known as the Sussex Tavern and now The Pantiles Hotel. It was here that Fanny Burney stayed with **Hester Thrale (1741-1821)** in 1778.

There is a further Heritage Plaque halfway down The Pantiles at No.44 to **Richard 'Beau' Nash (1674-1761),** the well known dandy and leader of fashion.

'Plaque for 'Beau' Nash at No.44 The Pantiles'

So concerned was he to keep up standards that he split his time between overseeing assemblies here and also in the town's eighteenth century rival, Bath. As the self-appointed Master of Ceremonies at Tunbridge Wells, he presided over balls in the former Assembly Rooms at Nos.40-46.

At the northern end of The Pantiles is what the spa is all about. The original Chalybeate Spring is here in front of the Bath House and each summer a 'dipper' ladles out water for all who wish to sample it. The Bath House you can see dates from 1804, but below it the original Cold Bath is still visible.

On leaving The Pantiles, cross Nevill Street, turn left and go down the small alley way, Cumberland Walk, on the right next to the Church of King Charles the Martyr. This church has played a significant part in the history of the spa. When the first visitors came here there was no place to worship and generous donations were given to remedy the situation. The names of **Samuel Pepys (1633-1703)** and **John Evelyn (1620-1706)**, who both visited here, are on the list of subscribers giving money for the building. Princess (later Queen) Victoria also attended church services here and a brass plaque marks her seat in the upper gallery.

Take the second set of steps on your left into Cumberland Gardens and at the end turn right up the hill past Jerningham House, one of the earliest lodging houses in the town. Continue up the hill along Mt. Sion. At No.63A is a Heritage Plaque to **Richard Cumberland**. In fact this playwright and novelist is also commemorated by Cumberland Walk and Cumberland Gardens through which you have just walked. His house, which no longer exists, must have been huge, extending from Nos.45 to 63 Mt. Sion.

'63A Mt.Sion, Richard Cumberland's House'

Turn left into Little Mt. Sion and then right into Belgrove, South Grove and then the High Street. (If you have young children with you, a few minutes spent in the children's play area in The Grove could be a good investment of time).

If adults want some respite from literary detective work as well then you're in the right place. The High Street is a lovely bridge between old and new Tunbridge Wells. Many buildings retain attractive Victorian fronts, housing a wide variety of modern shops and boutiques with lots of original items, designer clothes and restaurants. If old bookshops are your idea of heaven, you need to backtrack towards the Pantiles to the area in and around Chapel Place.

Still heading north, the High Street becomes Mount Pleasant Road after the Railway Station. On your left is Trinity Theatre. This imposing, neo Gothic building was originally Holy Trinity church, designed by Decimus Burton, and completed in 1829. The novelist and parodist, **Horace Smith (1779-1849)** spent his last years in Tunbridge Wells with his daughter Elizabeth and is buried in Holy Trinity churchyard.

Continue along Mount Pleasant Road to the next right, Monsoon Road. Here is The Tunbridge Wells Museum and Art Gallery, which is well worth a visit. The main collection actually dates from 1885, but it opened on this site in 1952 and gives a fascinating picture of what everyday life was like in Tunbridge Wells in past centuries. At the time of writing it is open daily with free admission.

Return to Mount Pleasant Road and continue walking north, turning left into Mount Ephraim Road. Look out for Thackeray's Restaurant at 85 London Road, on the edge of the Common and the corner of Mount Ephraim Road. **William Makepeace Thackeray** spent most of 1860 at this attractive tile hung house, then known as Rock Villa.

He gives a lovely description of the scene in front of you. "I stroll over the Common and survey the beautiful purple hills around, twinkling with a thousand bright villas, which have sprung up over this charming ground since I first saw it. What a delicious air breathes over the heath blows the cloud shadows across it and murmurs through the full clad trees. Can the world show a land, fairer, richer, more cheerful?" There is a Heritage Plaque to commemorate his stay.

From here, continue uphill on the footpath and cross London Road.

Be warned! It's a very busy road and great caution is advised. Belleville, the cottage where Thackeray spent part of his childhood, is here on a rocky slope. It is said that donkeys were once stabled below it.

With a brief diversion you can take in one more novelist before a well earned lunch. Continue south along Mount Ephraim turning right along Molyneux Park Road and then right again along Earls Road. There is a Heritage Plaque at No.10, Earls Road to mark where **E.M. Forster** lived from 1898-1901, while attending nearby Tonbridge School. Part of this afternoon's suggested itinerary will take you to his alma mater. It has a very distinguished list of Old Boys.

'No.10 Earls Road plaque for E.M.Forster'

To return to the Pantiles area it's probably simplest to just retrace your steps going back along Earls Road. Turn left into Molyneux Park Road to Mount Ephraim and then Mount Pleasant Road.

We suggest the afternoon is devoted to exploring the nearby old market town of Tonbridge. Apart from the distinguished Old Boys of Tonbridge School, the town has some interesting family links with **Jane Austen (1775-1817)**. Her father came from a long established Tonbridge family. There isn't, however, any concrete evidence that Jane herself ever actually visited the town.

Weirleigh, in Matfield, **Siegfried Sassoon's** ancestral home is 5 miles north east of Tunbridge Wells. (TN12 7DU). It is on your route. Take the A264 out of the town to join the A21 going south. Then take the B2160 to Matfield. Continue on the same road and drive through the village. After about half a mile from the centre of Matfield, you'll see the elaborate neo-Gothic house on the left hand side of the road. It's a surprisingly busy road so you need to keep a sharp look out. There are few places to stop in the vicinity.

There is also a strong local tradition-oral rather than written-which refers to it as 'The Haunted House'. **Robert Graves (1895-1985)**, at one stage at least, certainly believed this was the case. In 1929 in his largely autobiographical book, 'Goodbye to All That', he describes staying in the house in 1916, significantly not long after the death of Sassoon's younger brother at Gallipoli. He describes how he got very little sleep, being kept awake by "sudden rapping noises" and "diabolic yelling". Absolutely terrifying, but in this case at least there is probably a rational explanation.

It seems likely the dreadful sounds were made at a séance, held by Sassoon's mother desperate to communicate with her dead son. Graves, however, did not realise this and, as he wrote later "In the morning I told my friend 'I'm leaving this place, it's worse than France'". It was not until thirteen years after the incident that Graves wrote his account of it and in so doing deeply offended Sassoon. It caused a rift between the two former friends which lasted throughout their lives.

From here it is a very easy drive to Tonbridge. Just retrace your route, taking the B2160 back to the A21. It should then be a very quick drive north.

If you have a little more time we suggest a detour to the tiny village of Tudeley to track down not a writer but a great artist. All Saints parish church (TN11 ON2) is the only church in the world to have all twelve of its windows decorated by the great Russian-Jewish artist **Marc Chagall (1887-1985)**. There is a tragic story behind this. The windows are a memorial tribute to Sarah d'Avigdor Goldsmid, who died aged just 21 in a sailing accident off the Sussex coast at Rye. The family then lived in the village near the church.

The windows, with Chagall's trade mark brilliant colours, are inspirational and in spite of the great family sorrow which motivated them, they are full of joy and hope.

'The large stained glass window above the altar in Tudeley Church'

The simplest route to Tudeley from Matfield is again to retrace your route taking the B2160 back to the A21. On the outskirts of Tonbridge take the right hand road, B2017, signposted Tudeley and Paddock Wood. After visiting the church the same B2017 leads to the A26 and then Tonbridge. Alternatively just return to the A21 and continue north.

Once you do arrive in Tonbridge you will find there is ample parking and, like most old towns, it is best explored on foot.

A good landmark to head towards first is Tonbridge Castle (TN9 1BG). It lies just off Tonbridge High Street, inevitably in Castle Street and there are Pay and Display car parks situated next to it. It is reputedly England's finest example of a Motte and Bailey Castle with a superb 13th century gatehouse.

'Tonbridge Castle gatehouse'

In 1763 Mary Hooker, daughter of the castle's owner, was married to the Rev'd. Henry Austen, whose cousin George was Jane Austen's father. Yes, we agree it sounds a somewhat tenuous connection with the great novelist but, as you will note on your tour round the town, Jane's family links with the town were quite strong.

Leave the castle through the Gatehouse, following the path through the rose garden. Turn left by the public toilets (always useful to know where they are) and cross the road by the old fire station. Continue along Bank Street, past the shops and so join the High Street.

Pause first outside No.174 High Street. The eighteenth century building which stood here was destroyed by fire in 1997. At the time of writing the modern building on the site is a beauty salon. The original building was home to Jane Austen's grandfather, William Austen, a surgeon. Her father, George, lived here with his two sisters until her grandfather died in 1737 when her father was only six years old. One can only guess how traumatic this was for the young family. Their mother, Rebecca, had died two years earlier and their stepmother Susannah, while not actively cruel, does not seem to have liked young children. Jane's father, George, was sent to Tonbridge School, a family tradition.

The High Street could very well have been called Austen Street. The

Rev'd. Henry Austen and his wife Mary (from Tonbridge Castle) lived at number 182 with their five children, only three of whom survived infancy. At number 186 was Jane's great uncle, Thomas Austen, an apothecary and his family.

Carry on walking up the High Street, crossing the road at Lansdowne Road. Continue until you reach Tonbridge School founded in 1553. George Austen's time here just overlapped that of his cousin Henry, who was Head Boy when George started his distinguished career at the school. He went on to win a scholarship and bursary which enabled him to go to Oxford University. There is a blue plaque on the wall of the school's Cawthorn Lecture Theatre, erected by the Jane Austen (Kent) Society to commemorate the time spent here by her father, George Austen.

E.M. Forster was a pupil at the school in the 1890s. Sadly his time here was one of great unhappiness. He was bullied by the other boys and became deeply unhappy. How schools and society have changed. It is unlikely the twenty first century Tonbridge schoolboys would recognise what school days were like a hundred years ago. They would all, however, know the great novelist's name as there is a theatre named after him at the school.

In the 1930s **Sidney Keyes (1922-1943)** was a pupil here and some of the poems he wrote during his time at Tonbridge School were included in 'Iron Laurels' (1942) published while he was at Oxford. More recently **Frederick Forsyth**, **Tim Waterstone** and **Vikram Seth** are all distinguished Old Boys.

The large red building opposite the school is Ferox Hall (Ferox meaning the great lake trout). Today it is a boarding house for the school but in the eighteenth century it was owned by the Danvers family.

Their niece, Susannah Kelk, married Jane Austen's grandfather, William Austen and thus became stepmother to George Austen and his siblings.

'Ferox Hall'

Continue along the High Street and turn left into Church Lane and the Parish Church of St. Peter and St. Paul. Jane's grandfather, William, is buried in the north aisle, his grave covered by carpet for preservation.

As you leave the church, return to the High Street and you will see you are very close to Tonbridge Castle and probably where you parked your car.

TWO DAY VISIT

Five miles south of Tunbridge Wells is Groombridge Place, the ancestral home of the poet **Edmund Waller (1606-1687)**, who unsuccessfully wooed Lady Dorothy Sidney at nearby Penshurst Place. Her great uncle was the poet **Sir Philip Sidney (1554-1586)** and a very happy day can be passed exploring the homes of these two poets.

Groombridge Place (TN3 9PQ) straddles the border between Kent and Sussex. Its literary importance is not just because of its associations with the Waller family. **Conan Doyle (1859-1930)**, who lived in nearby

Crowborough, used it as a setting for several of his Sherlock Holmes stories.

Leave Tunbridge Wells via Mount Ephraim, on the A264 west bound, signposted East Grinstead. After five miles you will reach Ashhurst. Turn onto the B2100 for the pretty mile and a half drive to Groombridge. It's a very straightforward route clearly marked by brown signs. When you arrive watch out for friendly peacocks strutting around the car park.

The award winning formal Gardens at Groombridge Place are rumoured to have been designed in part by **John Evelyn.** They and the Enchanted Forest (Child Heaven) are open every day from 10.00am to 5.30pm from mid-March to the beginning of November. Although the house itself is closed to visitors there are two small buildings to look out for.

One building reproduces Sherlock Holmes' Baker Street study whilst elsewhere in the garden is a second building with a small exhibition centre filled with memorabilia of recent films shot here including 'Pride and Prejudice' and Peter Greenaway's 'The Draughtsman's Contract'.

As you walk through the grounds it would be a good idea to have a copy of Conan Doyle's 'The Valley of Fear' in your hand. In the story Holmes investigates a murder in Biristone Manor a "Jacobean brick house" which "rose upon the ruins of the feudal castle" surrounded by "an old fashioned garden of cut yews" on the "fringe of the great Weald Forest". Perhaps what really makes the Groombridge setting certain is that "the only approach to the house was over a drawbridge across a beautiful broad moat, as still and luminous as quicksilver in the cold winter sunshine".

One further detail may appeal to you after your drive here. While Dr.Watson strolls in the gardens, Sherlock Holmes ponders over the recently discovered dead body. Is it John Douglas or "the bicyclist from Tunbridge Wells?" All this evidence certainly seems to point to the story being set in Groombridge Place, which Conan Doyle visited often from his nearby home in Crowborough. Here at Groombridge he would take part in séances with the owners Louisa and Eliza Saint.

'Groombridge Place, moat and swans'

For more information go to the website at www.groombridge.co.uk or telephone 01892 861444

Five hundred years ago Groombridge Place was the home of the Waller family. When the young poet **Edmund Waller (1606-1687)** stayed here with relations, he unsuccessfully wooed Lady Dorothy, "fair Sacharissa" in the poems, at nearby Penshurst Place (TN11 8DG). You could make this your second visit of the day – it's a very simple journey between the two houses.

For information about this remarkable ancestral house, today the home of Viscount De L'Isle, see www.penshurstplace.com or telephone 01892 870307. You'll find it is open daily from the end of March to the end of October and at weekends at other times in the year.

To get there return to the A264 at Ashhurst and turn east for Tunbridge Wells. Just before Langton Green join the B2188 for Penshurst. Again it is very well sign posted so just follow the brown signs.

Lady Dorothy Sidney received dozens of poems addressed to her from Edmund Waller. While walking about the estate he wrote:

"Ye lofty beeches, tell the matchless dame
That if together ye fed all our flame

131

It could not equalise the hundredth part
Of what her eyes have kindled in my heart"

It's worth hunting out the "matchless dame's" portrait which hangs in the house to see whether you agree with the love-lorn poet. You'll notice, however, it is not labelled Dorothy Waller. Sadly for Edmund, Dorothy succumbed to the charms of one of the great aristocrats of the time and married Lord Spencer (later Earl of Sunderland). She became mistress of Althorp which, five hundred years later, became Princess Diana's childhood home.

Dorothy's great uncle, the poet and Elizabethan courtier **Sir Philip Sidney**, was born here more than seventy years earlier in 1554. His love poems to his adored Stella (in real life Penelope Devereux) is the first great sonnet sequence in English. It was to be another unhappy love story as Penelope was married, much against her will, to Lord Rich. (You may have noticed all the photographs in this book were taken by *Michael* Rich but, very sadly, we have not been able to trace an aristocratic lineage for him!).

Sir Philip Sidney had inherited the estate while he was Governor of Flushing. Shortly afterwards, in 1586, mortally wounded in the Battle of Zutphen, he selflessly gave his water bottle to another dying soldier with the memorable words: "Thy necessity is yet greater than mine". This nobility confirmed the reputation he had in his lifetime of being the perfect Renaissance courtier. Learned and polite, but also generous and brave, although he was only 31 on his death his place in history was ensured.

Penshurst Place has seen many distinguished writers in its time. **Ben Jonson (1572-1637)** was a frequent visitor and in 'To Penshurst' from 'The Forest' (1612) he describes the groves, the river and the oak tree planted when Sir Philip Sidney was born. Then he paints a vivid word picture of the house exterior covered in fruit bushes:

"The blushing apricot and woolly peach
Hang on thy walls that every child may reach"

John Evelyn was here in the summer of 1652 doing the same as you and visiting from nearby Tunbridge Wells. He wrote in his diary that the place was: "famous once for its gardens and excellent fruit and for the noble conversation which was wont to be had there". That seems to confirm what Jonson had thought forty years earlier and we certainly recommend a visit to the Gardens today. With their variety of form, foliage and bloom they are lovely throughout the year.

IF YOU HAVE MORE TIME

You may want to fit in another garden after seeing the glories of Groombridge and Penshurst Place. If you have the luxury of more time why not pick up part of the suggested Tenterden trail, which is very close to here and spend a day at Sissinghurst. You won't regret it. It is about ten miles away, giving the opportunity for another interesting literary detour.

Take the A264 out of Tunbridge Wells to join the A21 southbound and then the A262 eastbound. Turn off to the left onto the B2079 at Goudhurst for a brief diversion to Curtisden Green.

The poet and novelist, **Richard Church (1893-1972)** lived here between 1939 and 1965, near the post office at The Oast House. Two volumes of his autobiography 'Over the Bridge' and 'The Golden Sovereign' were published during his time here as well as 'A Solitary Man and Other Poems'.

If you then rejoin the B262 you are just four miles from Sissinghurst Castle Garden, restored from 1930 by **Vita Sackville-West (1892-1962)** and her husband, **Harold Nicolson (1886-1968)**. Many would say this is the loveliest garden in England.

CAN I DO THESE TOURS WITHOUT A CAR?

Yes you can.

Royal Tunbridge Wells is less than an hour by train from London Charing Cross, Gatwick Airport and Ashford International railway station. More information can be found by calling 08457 484950.

BEST TIME TO VISIT

Tunbridge Wells is situated in the unspoilt beauty of the Weald, designated an Area of Outstanding Natural Beauty and is lovely in different ways throughout the year. Obviously the profusion of colour in Gardens such as Groombridge Place and Sissinghurst is best seen in Spring and Summer.

Autumn in the Weald can rival New England in the Fall.

And if you want real spa treatment, a costumed 'dipper' serves out the original Chalybeate Spring Water in the traditional manner during the summer months in The Pantiles.

IF YOU HAVE CHILDREN

On the afternoon of the Day One Tour we suggest you park your car at Tonbridge Castle (TN9 1BG). Why not fit in a visit to the castle before you pick up the literary trail again. It's somewhere that history really comes alive with its interactive displays, life size figures, special effects and dramatic lighting. For more information telephone 01732 770929 or go to www.tonbridgecastle.org.

On Day Two, as you explore Groombridge Place and Penshurst Place, why not let youngsters loose in the ancient woodland of 'The Enchanted Forest' at Groombridge Place (TN3 9PQ). There is adventure and mystery here for all ages with added extras of flying displays by birds of prey and canal boat cruises. More information is available on 01892 861444 or www.groombridge.co.uk

A fifteen minute drive north of Tunbridge Wells on the A228 at Paddock Wood is the Hop Farm Family Park (TN12 6PY). It could be a short detour from seeing Siegfried Sassoon's house at Matfield. The farm park is also easily accessible by the No.6 bus from Tunbridge Wells and Tonbridge which runs every hour.

Once the young back seat passengers have been treated to the adventure playground and the crazy golf, not to mention the Pirate Cove and 4D cinema, you should have no trouble in negotiating a good deal of uninterrupted literary detective work. Much more information is available on www.thehopfarm.co.uk or telephone 01622 872068.

SEVENOAKS

"And if six green oak trees should accidentally fall..."

Local historians believe that Sevenoaks' name is self-explanatory: it derives from a clearing with seven oak trees. This clearing may have been where the Dartford road (now the High Street) joined the main road from London. A market grew up where the roads met and then a town called Seovenaka by the Saxons which, in time, mutated to Sevenoaks.

Even today some market stalls can still be seen outside the Chequers pub on Saturday mornings. Another possible candidate for the town name could be the seven oaks growing near a small chapel in Knole Park. Over the centuries these trees have been replanted in the same spot several times but in the great storm of 1987 six of the most recent were blown down. This led some wags to suggest the town should be renamed Oneoak. Somehow it doesn't have the same ring to it.

SEVENOAKS' WRITERS

Sir Winston Churchill (1874-1965)

It is for his brilliant leadership during World War II that Churchill is best remembered but, for the purpose of this book, it is the statesman's 'off duty' work that is significant. He and his family lived in Chartwell, south of Sevenoaks, for 41 years and much of that time was given over to writing. The fruits of his writing are there for all to see. With the income generated he was able to enlarge and improve the garden, build a tennis court, brick walls, a swimming pool and an island in the lake.

'Churchill statue on Westerham Green'

His books brought him more than just financial success. In 1953 he was awarded the Nobel Prize for Literature, although it is probably his slightly later 'A History of the English Speaking Peoples' in 4 volumes (1956-1958), which has received most critical acclaim.

Edward Thomas (1878-1917)

Born in Lambeth and proud of his Welsh heritage, Philip Edward Thomas nevertheless spent a major part of his life in Kent, first moving at the time of his marriage in 1901 to Bearsted (see the Maidstone chapter). Between 1904 and 1906 the family rented Else's Farm at Sevenoaks Weald, three miles south of Sevenoaks. Although Thomas's lasting fame has come from his poetry it was as a critic that he tried to support his family. He told friends that he frequently spent 16 hours a day on reviews and other commissions but, in spite of this, he always seemed to be short of money.

His home became quite a centre for writers with a number of his literary friends, including **Edward Garnett (1868-1937)** and his son **David Garnett (1892-1981),** spending weekends there. But most gossip in the village may have centred on **W.H. Davies (1871-1940)**, who spent several months writing 'Autobiography of a Super Tramp' in Stidolph's Cottage on the farmland. While there, Davies broke his wooden leg (one might speculate how but the full details are not recorded) and the village carpenter had to make a temporary replacement from Thomas's design.

Vita Sackville-West (1892-1962)

The novelist, poet and gardener (she would probably have placed 'gardener' as her primary achievement) the Hon. Victoria Mary Sackville-West, Lady Nicholson, is best known as Vita Sackville-West. She was born in 1892 at Knole House, the home of her parents Lord and Lady Sackville. She followed in the long line of literary Sackvilles and started writing poetry at a very young age.

'Knole House'

In 1913 she married the diplomat Harold Nicolson and they moved to Constantinople. On their return to England the following year they bought Long Barn in nearby Sevenoaks Weald, but it was the move to

Sissinghurst (see the Tenterden chapter) which gave full vent to Vita's gardening genius.

She adored Knole, the home of her ancestors, but being a woman she was debarred from inheriting the estate, even though she was her parents' only child (bitterly, she referred to her gender as "a technical fault").

After her father's death in 1930, the house passed to her uncle Edward Sackville-West, the nearest male relative. With great honesty she wrote to him: "I suppose my love for Knole has gone deeper than anything else in my life" and this intense longing is evident in much of her writing. Thinly disguised, Knole became Chevron in her novel 'The Edwardians', written in 1930, the year she lost what she felt was her rightful inheritance. She had earlier written about her family history in fascinating detail in 'Knole and the Sackvilles' (1922).

Andy Pandy and his friends (created 1951)

Geographical proximity throws up some strange bed-fellows. Among the famous poets and novelists, who spent substantial parts of their lives in Sevenoaks and district, were the originators of the TV puppets which figured hugely in the childhoods of those born in the middle of the twentieth century. Who can say which imaginative creations have had the greatest long term influence?

Five miles south of Sevenoaks, in the lovely small town of Westerham, several inhabitants were responsible for developing Andy Pandy, the little boy dressed in a cut down stripy clown's outfit, as well as his friends Teddy and Looby Loo, the rag doll. Later the team went on to produce The Flowerpot Men and the delightful Woodentops.

The initial idea came from artist, writer and Westerham resident **Freda Lingstrom (1893-1989)** who was appointed Assistant Head of Schools Broadcasting in 1947. Together with her friend, the author-composer **Maria Bird**, she created Andy Pandy when she became Head of BBC Children's Television in 1951.The two set up Westerham Arts Films. One feels certain that those original films with Andy Pandy's best friend Teddy and later Bill and Ben were shot in glorious technicolour. Such is the power of the imagination. In fact all 26 of the original episodes of 'Andy Pandy' were shot in black and white. Colour episodes did not appear until 1970. 'The Flowerpot Men' had to wait till 2000 before they changed black and white for colour.

It was another Westerham family who actually breathed life into the puppets. **Audrey Atterbury (1921-1997)** was heavily involved in The Westerham Press, which her husband Rowley had founded in the village in 1949. The following year she found herself sitting next to Freda Lingstrom on the London train. They started chatting and by the end of the journey Audrey had been persuaded to become a puppeteer for the new television series of 'Andy Pandy'. It was to be the start of an exciting change of career for Audrey, who later worked for the Little Angel Theatre, one of Britain's leading puppet theatres.

And perhaps that surname 'Atterbury' sounds a little familiar. There were persistent rumours, never confirmed or denied, that Freda Lingstrom modelled the appearance of Andy Pandy on Audrey's young son Paul, born in 1945. He was 6 years old when the first programme was screened. He grew up to become an antiques expert (one of his prized possessions is the only remaining Teddy puppet from the TV series that is not part of a museum collection.) Today he still appears regularly on the BBC as an expert on The Antiques Roadshow. An amazing series of coincidences.

ONE DAY VISIT

Sevenoaks is more than just an attractive setting for Knole, although the majestic fifteenth century house certainly dominates the literary history of the town. Edmund Burke actually declared that: "Knole is the most interesting thing in England". Many other writers have visited the town and sites connected with them are well worth discovering. We suggest you start in the town centre at South Park car park, behind the Stag Community Arts Centre, Theatre & Cinema (01732 450175) and spend a morning hunting out several other writers on your way to Knole.

As you exit the car park along Buckhurst Lane you will see a small Tourist Information Centre which may be worth a visit. For information before your visit call 01732 450305 or log on to www.sevenoakstown. gov.uk. Whether you turn left or right here you will find interesting literary sites.

'23 Eardley Road with a plaque for H.G.Wells'

If you turn left, less than a ten minute walk along London Road will bring you to the junction with Eardley Road. Turn left into this and seek out No.23 (TN13 1XX) – it's almost opposite St. Luke's church. There is a blue plaque outside the house to commemorate H.G Wells' year long stay here in 1894. Born in Bromley (thinly disguised as Bromstead in 'The New Machiavelli') in 1866, Wells' first profession was teaching but he caused a great scandal by running away with one of his students.

They lived together here at 23 Eardley Road with her mother, though there must have been many tensions in the household. The girl's mother disliked him so much that she could not bring herself to eat with him. The lack of socialising may have given him some spare time and perhaps this was beneficial to his writing career. As the plaque states, it was while living in this house that Wells wrote 'The Time Machine', believed by many to be the first English language science fiction story.

A year later, in 1895, Wells and Catherine (always known as Jane) Robbins were married and in 1896 moved to Sandgate near Folkestone. Have a look at the Dover chapter to continue Wells' story.

Retrace your steps (though you might find it simpler to drive to Eardley Road before parking in South Park car park) and this time turn right at the Stag Theatre.

'Red House'

Three buildings beyond Waitrose supermarket, behind the red post box, is The Red House, the offices of a firm of solicitors. This handsome house was built in 1686 for Dr.Fuller, a pharmacist and in time became the home of Dr.Francis Austen, great-uncle of Jane Austen. Her great grandmother, Elizabeth Austen, had been housekeeper to the headmaster of nearby Sevenoaks School. Look out for the Sevenoaks Preservation Society plaque on the railings which commemorates the Austen connection.

Jane herself stayed at The Red House in 1788 but the novelist's associations with the area do not stop there. She is believed to have partly based Rosings Park, the home of the formidable Lady Catherine de Burgh in 'Pride and Prejudice', on Chevening House (TN14 6HG), outside Sevenoaks near Westerham. One of her many cousins was Rector of Chevening and it is certainly recorded that she stayed at least once with him.

Perhaps his parsonage became the inspiration for Hunsford Rectory but surely she couldn't have been so unkind as to model the odious Mr Collins on her cousin.

Today, this grand house is the official residence of the Foreign Secretary and is not open to the public, although the grounds are usually opened several times a year for charity. For more information on this call 01732 744809 or go to info@cheveninghouse.com

Continue straight along the High Street and when you are opposite the gate to Knole turn right into St Nicholas churchyard. Two of Charles Dickens' daughters are buried here. The novelist made one recorded visit to Sevenoaks when he rented an apartment nearby in Seale House close to Vine Tavern. A few years after his death, his daughter Katey and her second husband, the artist Carlo Perugini, came to live in Sevenoaks, first staying at the White Hart Inn on the Tonbridge Road and then renting Park Cottage two hundred yards further up the hill.

'St.Nicholas Church and a plaque to John Donne in the pavement'

The side entrance to the church is usually open. Between 1616 and his death in 1631 the rector was the poet **John Donne (1572-1631)**. At the same time he was also Dean of St Paul's Cathedral in London. His responsibilities for the spiritual welfare of the ordinary people of Sevenoaks do not seem to have over concerned him. Although an annual guest at Knole, where he preached each time in the chapel, there isn't any evidence of his preaching at or even visiting the church at the end of the drive.

You will find a coffee shop and toilets in the Undercroft of the church. Both are usually open on weekday lunchtimes.

Now it is time to visit one of the glories of Kent, originally owned by Thomas Bourchain, Archbishop of Canterbury, in 1456. It is certainly an excellent reason to make Sevenoaks your centre for a few days' exploration.

'White Hart feeding in Knole Park'

The entrance to Knole House (TN15 0RP) is opposite the church. Set in the midst of a medieval deer park and the seat of the Sackville family since the 16th century, it is more of a stately hamlet than a private house. It is a 'Calendar House' with 365 rooms, 52 staircases and 7 courtyards and is the largest house cared for by the National Trust. The long-time owners, the Sackvilles, seem to have possessed strong literary genes and the house has seen a succession of writers and their patrons over the centuries. **Sir Thomas Sackville, first Earl of Dorset (1536-1608)**, was a court poet and joint author of 'Gorboduc' (1565), one of the first English dramas. The year after its publication he was given the house by his cousin Queen Elizabeth I.

In the following century the third earl was a friend to several poets including **Ben Jonson (1572-1637), John Fletcher (1579-1625), Michael Drayton (1563-1631)** and, especially, the Rector of St. Nicholas between 1616 and 1631, **John Donne**.

The sixth Earl of Dorset, **Charles Sackville (1638-1706)** was himself the author of several lyrics and satires. Probably the most notorious, and bravest, were those on James II's mistress, Lady Dorchester:

"Can any dress find a way
To stop the approaches of decay

And mend a ruined face?
Cans't thou forget thy age and pox?
Can all that shines on shells and rocks
Make thee a fine young thing?"

Brave words indeed to write about such a well connected lady but his sparkling wit and popularity seem to have saved him and there wasn't any come back from the King.

Samuel Pepys (1633-1703), always one to know the hot gossip of the day, wrote that in his youth the sixth earl was a close friend of Charles II. He kept "a merry house" at Epsom "with a pretty young orange seller named Nell Gwynn." It was not long before she moved on to become the King's mistress. Charles Sackville was also a friend of and patron to many leading poets of his day.

One was **John Dryden (1631-1700)** who became the first Poet Laureate in 1668. Later, Sackville used his influence to secure the same post for **Thomas Shadwell (1642-1692)**. A frequent visitor to Knole was **Matthew Prior (1624-1721)** who, tellingly, described being entertained there: "A freedom reigned at his table which made every one of his guests think himself at home. His good nature was supreme." That dining-room became known as the Poets' Parlour because it had so many portraits of poets on the wall.

The most famous Sackville writer was the one who, being a woman, could not inherit the estate. Knole was **Vita Sackville-West's** much loved birthplace and home until her marriage to Harold Nicolson in 1913. Of her beloved childhood home she wrote: "It has the deep inward gaiety of some very old woman who has always been beautiful, who has had many lovers and seen generations come and go, smiled wisely over their sorrows and their joys and learnt an imperishable secret of tolerance and humour".

Of course it was another woman writer who made sure that Knole will always have a unique place in literature. In the 1920s Vita was romantically involved with **Virginia Woolf (1882-1941)** who, in 1928 celebrated the house in 'Orlando', a time travelling novel (in fact the author preferred the category of biography rather than novel for the book).

She based the gender-shifting hero on Vita as a tribute to their

ardent relationship. At the early planning stage it was even proposed that one illustration for the book would be a photograph of Vita dressed in the style of a Lely portrait and seated inside a large gilded frame. In this novel/biography at least, Vita had her heart's desire and became the once and future heir of her beloved Knole.

Since 1947 the property has been shared between the Sackville-West family and the National Trust. When Vita was required to sign documents relinquishing any claims on the property she wrote: "The signing nearly broke my heart...I regarded it as a betrayal of all the tradition of my ancestors and the house I loved". She did, however, relent sufficiently to write the first National Trust guidebook to the house in 1948.

Today the Sackville-West family still live in the house and own most of the deer park. Normal National Trust opening times operate. For more information call 01732 450608 or look up www.nationaltrust. org.uk

It might be a nice idea to have one of those famous National Trust lunches at Knole but you will also be able to find many pleasant places to eat in Sevenoaks itself.

We suggest that a major part of the afternoon is given over to another National Trust property, Churchill's beloved Chartwell. It is located just outside Westerham, five miles west of Sevenoaks with its wealth of literary and historical connections. The parish covers about 17 square miles and, amazingly, the small town itself, covering barely half a square mile, contains more than 140 listed buildings. It's well worth a visit.

But first drive south out of Sevenoaks for three miles to the village of Sevenoaks Weald. It's a straightforward journey along the High Street past Sevenoaks School to the A21. Go through Riverhead then at the roundabout take the exit marked Weald. **Edward Thomas (1878-1917)** came here in 1904 and lived on the outskirts of the village (today about 300 yards from the A21) on Morleys Road at Else's Farm, near the railway bridge and opposite the pub (TN14 6QR).

In his day this was known as The Shant but at the time of writing it has been renamed, rather appropriately, Edwards Bar and Brassiere (call 01732 443687 for more information). Thomas also rented Stidolph's Cottage in Eggpie Lane as a writing retreat. It is said that in the two years the family lived in the village he wore a path out in the fields between farmhouse and cottage as he went between the two several times a day.

Thomas spent a weekend listening to his friend, the writer and tramp, **W.H. Davies (1871-1940)**, sitting by the farmhouse fire recounting his experiences on the road in America and seeking his fortune in the Klondike Gold Rush. Thomas knew these extraordinary adventures deserved a wider audience and installed him in the cottage to write 'The Autobiography of a Super Tramp', which was eventually published in 1908.

'Elses Farm plaque on its gatepost'

From Sevenoaks Weald it is an easy journey first to Westerham and then to Chartwell, Churchill's home just outside the town. Take the lane signposted Sevenoaks and join the A225. A mile further on turn onto the A225 then take the A25 to Westerham.

The best starting point for exploration is probably on The Green. There are two statues at either end remembering two great patriots but their styles are very different. That to General James Wolfe, who was born and brought up in Westerham, is a traditional tribute to a conquering hero. This great man seized Quebec from the French. His home is east of the centre of Westerham opposite Quebec house.

At the opposite end of The Green there is a massive brooding bronze statue of **Sir Winston Churchill** by Oscar Nemon, with the simple words Churchill and the great man's dates, 1874-1965. There is a plaque on the rough-hewn stone plinth telling that it was presented by Marshall Tito and the people of Yugoslavia in homage to Churchill's leadership in the Second World War.

Tucked into a corner north of the village green, is the 800 year old parish church of St. Mary, the Virgin (TN16 1AS). **John Fryth (1503-1533)**, an English martyr, was born in Westerham and baptized here. He went on to help Tyndale translate the Bible into English but his life finished early when only thirty, he was burnt at the stake in Smithfield as a heretic. There is a memorial window by Burne Jones in his memory in the church.

Outside in the graveyard is the final resting place of **Noel Streatfeild (1895-1986)**, the author of so many popular children's books (and that is the correct spelling of her surname; memorize that and you could win your next pub quiz!). For much more information about her in the county of her birth, have a look at our companion book 'Follow these Writers...in SUSSEX'.

A leaflet is available inside the church showing the location of named graves (including that of Peter Nissen, who gave his name to the corrugated hut he designed which gave civilians so much protection in WWII).

Return to the village green and on the south side, virtually opposite Churchill's statue but across the road (here called Vicarage Lane), is Breaches, a large Tudor house.

'Breaches, Westerham Village Green'

This became home to **Alice Liddell (1852-1934)**, a clue being in her first name. The Liddell family were friends of **Lewis Carroll** (real name Charles Dodgson), an Oxford Mathematics professor. One summer holiday he took the 10 year old Alice and two of her sisters, boating on the Thames and entertained them with a story of the girl who fell down a rabbit hole. Alice loved the story and insisted he wrote it down. Three years later, in 1865, 'Alice's Adventures in Wonderland' was published.

Alice later married the cricketer Reginald Hargreaves and spent her final years at Breaches. Her Rolls Royce (number plate A1) might occasionally be seen parked by the stable block, now renamed Owl House. She died here in 1934 but her ashes are buried in the churchyard of St Michael's Church in Lyndhurst in the New Forest, where she had lived for much of her life.

Westerham has one more connection with a very famous book. Westerham Place, formerly known as Darenth Towers, was the home of **Luke Hansard (1752-1828)**. This printer gave his name to the daily record of Parliamentary business which he was the first to produce.

While you are in the centre of the town it is worth glancing up to the floor above the present chemist's shop. The two notorious Soviet spies,

Burgess and MacLean, owned a flat there and, in those pre-digital days, used a darkroom in it to develop their films.

Two miles south of Westerham is Chartwell and the house (TN16 1PS) that takes its name from the district. Turn left at Breaches along Hosey Hill then right onto the A2026 signposted Edenbridge. Chartwell is clearly signposted.

'Chartwell'

Sir Winston Churchill bought the house, its farm and the surrounding 80 acres in 1922 for £5,000. Much work needed to be done and the family was not able to move in for another two years. Philip Tilden, the most sought after architect of the day, was commissioned to remodel and extend it. He later wrote: "No client that I have ever had has ever spent more time trouble or interest in the making of his home than did Mr.Churchill." It became an exceptionally happy environment for the great man. "I never had a dull or idle moment from morning to midnight and with my happy family around me dwelt at peace within my habitation", he wrote. So happy was he here that he spent most of his out of office years in the 1930s at Chartwell, gardening, painting and entertaining.

Although he stipulated absolute quiet from his family while he was writing (how many other writers might read those words a little wistfully), at other times there were great family parties, especially at Christmas time with charades and theatrical performances in the dining room. There is a Visitors Book just inside the front door signed by family and friends, political figures and celebrities from all round the world.

Churchill even took up brick laying, becoming so highly skilled, that the local shop steward for the building trade union wanted to recruit him. Sadly that imaginative proposal was vetoed by the Union's National Executive.

Above all he spent his time here writing. 'The World Crisis', 'Marlborough' - a life of his ancestor the Duke - and 'The History of the English Speaking Peoples' were all produced at Chartwell.

A group of wealthy businessmen bought the house for the nation in 1946 with the stipulation that it should pass to the National Trust following the deaths of both Sir Winston and his wife. In fact Lady Clementine Churchill graciously vacated the house on her husband's death in 1965.

Normal National Trust opening times operate, although the Garden, Shop and Restaurant are also open in winter time. For more information go to www.nationaltrust.org.uk/chartwell or telephone 01732 868381

Virtually next door to Chartwell, on Mapleton Road, is Chartwell Cottage. This was home to Andy Pandy's creator **Freda Lingstrom**. She lived here with the TV character's co-creator **Maria Bird**. It was a platonic relationship. Both women had lost their fiancés in World War I.

It's now a straightforward return, first retracing the route to Westerham and then taking the A25 to Sevenoaks. You could feel this is a very full itinerary for one day and if you have the luxury of more time in the area you could easily spread it over at least two days.

TWO DAY VISIT

Today's exploration is to the north of Sevenoaks.

We suggest you first take the A21 north west out of Sevenoaks through Riverhead for 5 miles to Halstead. The children's writer **Edith**

Nesbit (1858-1924) spent three of her teenage years with her family at Halstead Hall.

"A long low red-brick house that might have been commonplace but for the roses and the ivy that clung to the front of it and the rich heavy jasmine that covered the side", as she later described it. In those quieter days of the 1870s she and her brothers and sisters frequently played around the new railway line at nearby Knockholt (now on the busy A21) and this experiences almost certainly gave her some material for her 1906 novel 'The Railway Children'.

Edith Nesbit is further distinguished as one of the founders, along with her husband, of the Fabian Society in 1884. Their son Fabian was named after the Society.

Close to there, off the A225, is the pretty village of Shoreham. In his final years the poet and painter **William Blake (1757-1827)** had a good deal of influence over a group of young painters in this area, especially Samuel Palmer who moved to Water House in Shoreham in 1826, the year before Blake's death. Blake made several visits to Water House, joining the young painters on their day and night tramps over the surrounding countryside, reciting poetry as they went.

He even accompanied them on a ghost hunt to the village's ruined castle. Their admiration for him grew when he showed his supposed telepathic powers by foretelling Palmer's unexpected appearance some time before it happened.

To see where all this happened, turn left off the A225 at Shoreham station along Station Road. The village itself is quite tucked away. Turn left again at the church and then right along Darenth Way.

Water House, a handsome building surprisingly not built near the riverside, is straight in front of you. There is a plaque on the wall outside stating **Samuel Palmer (artist) 1805-1884** lived and worked here 1827-1834/5. Certainly he worked at the house but there is some disagreement among historians as to whether he actually lived here. Some believe that he lived in a nearby rundown cottage and it was his father who rented Water House. Whichever is true it would certainly be good to believe that Blake took his inspiration for 'Jerusalem' from one of his many walks in the glorious surrounding countryside.

On the outskirts of the village is Dunstall Priory (TN14 7UE), the childhood home of **Lord Dunsany (1878-1957)**. This is private property and is not open to visitors. The Anglo-Irish writer of plays, short stories and verses lies buried in Shoreham churchyard. During World War II the Priory became associated with another eminent writer. **Anthony Powell CH (1905-2000)** was engaged in intelligence work at the War Office and spent his free time visiting his family living here.

And now we suggest you allow yourself plenty of time for the main focus of the day. Eight miles north west of Sevenoaks is the village of Downe (BR6 7JT), site of Down (confusingly without the village's final 'e') House where **Charles Darwin (1809-1882)** wrote 'On the Origin of the Species'.

From Shoreham briefly drive south to join the A224 and then drive north again on this road. Turn left onto the A21 and continue for about 4 miles following signs to Down.

Charles Darwin and his wife, Emma, a member of the illustrious Wedgwood family, lived here with their ten children for 40 years until Charles' death in 1882. He loved the house: "I think I was never in a more perfectly quiet country", he wrote and he became a pillar of local society, enjoying his garden and welcoming visitors.

One of these frequent visitors was the satirist and novelist **Samuel Butler (1835-1902)**. In 'Unconscious Memory' (1880) Butler describes a fierce disagreement which developed between them. There were to be no more visits.

Life at Down House has also been immortalized by Charles Darwin's granddaughter, the writer and wood engraver **Gwen Raverat (1885-1957)** who was born 3 years after her grandfather's death. Her 1952 book 'Period Piece', which she both wrote and illustrated, is an infectiously happy book of childhood memoirs. She describes the idiosyncrasies of her five Darwin uncles and conveys the feel of family holidays in Kent. Touchingly, she says: "To us everything at Down was perfect."

'Down House'

Down House is now owned by English Heritage and much has been done to make Darwin's ground breaking work accessible to all, with a detailed full scale replica of his cabin on board HMS Beagle and a fascinating exhibition charting his life and scientific work. The house has extensive gardens which proved the inspiration for much of Darwin's work. It is possible to follow in his footsteps along the Sandwalk - what he famously termed his "thinking path". For more information visit www.english-heritage.org.uk/darwin or call 01689 859119.

To return to Sevenoaks a rather quicker way than you came, follow directions to Biggin Hill on the A233 and continue south to Westerham. If you have more free time you might find it worthwhile to travel further north to Bromley on the outskirts of London where two very different novelists made their homes.

H.G. Wells (1866-1946) (those initials stand for Herbert George) was born here and as we saw in the One Day Visit, he spent a momentous year in Sevenoaks writing 'The Time Machine'. He later wrote a short story called 'Miss Winchelsea's Heart', where the eponymous heroine's hopes are dashed when she discovers the object of her affections is called Mr.Snooks. "All the refinement she had figured was ruined and defaced by that cognomen's inexorable vulgarity".

Perhaps a little harsh and certainly more than a little snobbish, the modern reader might conclude.

She is so disgusted at the thought of becoming Mrs.Snooks that she rebuffs all advances made by her beloved, although irritatingly she never tells him the reason for her actions. Not surprisingly he turns his attentions instead to her friend Fanny. In a letter to our snobbish heroine, Fanny explains what the surname actually means. "It means Sevenoaks only it has got down to Snooks. Both Snooks and Noakes, dreadfully vulgar surnames though they be, are really worn forms of Sevenoaks. So I said "if it got down from Sevenoaks to Snooks why not get it back from Snooks to Sevenoaks?"

It makes a neatly told story - clever Fanny gets her man and Miss Winchelsea is left to lament her excessive snobbery - but it is difficult to verify the name derivation Fanny so confidently states.

Another Bromley resident was **Richmal Crompton Lamburn 1890-1969)**. She dropped the final surname when she came to write her 'Just William' books about that endearingly naughty schoolboy. Like H.G.Wells she too first earned her living as a schoolteacher. While living at 9 Cherry Orchard Road she combined teaching classics at Bromley High School for Girls with writing the first 'Just William' books. In 1923 aged 34 she contracted poliomyelitis and lost the use of her right leg. She felt unable to continue teaching.

What must have been a dreadful period for her was also a great gift to the literary world. She took up writing full time and was so successful that she had The Glebe built for herself and her mother in Oakley Road, Bromley. She later moved to Chislehurst, her final home.

IF YOU HAVE MORE TIME

Ightham Mote (TN15 0NT), a beautiful moated 14th century Manor House in the small village of Ivy Hatch, lies six miles south east of Sevenoaks. It was used by the American historical novelist **Anya Seton (1904-1990)** in her 1972 romance 'Green Darkness'.

This fascinating time switching story tells of a modern couple plagued by their earlier incarnations in Tudor England. Use is made of the legend of a walled up skeleton behind a blocked door and one has a sense of dread when the heroine, Celia de Bohun, comes searching for her beloved in "the lovely and mysterious manor".

The original house had made a great impression on the writer when she visited it in the 1960s shortly after it had been bought and restored from ruins by the American Charles Henry Robinson. He was later to present it to the National Trust.

A very straightforward drive easterly from Sevenoaks along the A25 takes you to this exquisite house.

'Ightham Mote - side view with Mote (moat)'

Normal National Trust opening hours operate but much more information about visiting this lovely house is available by calling 01732 810378 ext.100 or by visiting www.nationaltrust.org.uk/ighthammote

The Plough (TN15 0NL) is virtually next door to the entrance to Ightham Mote. We suggest you fortify yourself here with lunch before completing the day's detective work. No frozen or pre-made dishes are served here and purely in the interest of research we have tried quite a number - all absolutely delicious. For more information telephone 01732 810100 or visit www.theploughivyhatch.co.uk)

CAN I DO THESE TOURS WITHOUT A CAR?

Sevenoaks has all the advantages and disadvantages of a commuter town on the London fringe, since it is 20 miles south east of Charing Cross on one of the principal commuter rail links to and from the capital. Contact National Rail enquiries on 08457 484950 for more information about this and also for details of Edenbridge Station for Chartwell, Borough Green and Wrotham stations for Ightham Mote.

A word of warning though. Don't spend time looking for Westerham station. It doesn't exist, although it did so once upon a time. It was closed on 28th October 1961 as part of rail reorganization and some of the track now lies buried beneath the M25 north of the town.

You should find more than one bus to take you between the sites mentioned. Southdown PSV236 Westerham to East Grinstead goes to within ½ mile of Chartwell and New Enterprise 404 from Sevenoaks goes close to Ightham Mote. Public transport information is available on 0871 200 22 33or www.traveline.info.

BEST TIME TO VISIT

An annual Sevenoaks Literary Celebration is held every autumn and is in its 10th year at the time of writing. More information on this interesting event is available from the organisers: Sevenoaks Bookshop on 01732 452055

Since the suggested itineraries involve the three National Trust properties of Chartwell, Knole and Ightham Mote it seems sensible to plan your visit between Easter and late October when all three are open.

One interesting footnote to this is that **Octavia Hill (1838-1912)**, the remarkable co-founder of the National Trust, was another Westerham resident. Her health was damaged by her intensive charity work in London helping the poor. Consequently she and her companion and helper, Harriot Yorke, then moved to Larksfield in Crockham Hill, south of Westerham After her death in 1912 she was buried at Holy Trinity Church, Crockham Hill.

IF YOU HAVE CHILDREN

Several of the suggested literary sites also offer good facilities for children. In our experience youngsters love both wandering about in the medieval deer park at Knole and also imagining themselves back 'in the olden days' at Ightham Mote. The latter has an excellent children's trail to try out.

English Heritage, the administrators of Down House, have worked hard to make this fascinating home as family friendly as possible. Older children especially will enjoy the interactive digital presentation of Darwin's Beagle diary and notebooks and in the garden the amazing carnivorous plants he studied in the hot house should certainly meet with approval.

For something that is specifically designed for a family day out remember The Hop Farm Family Park (TN12 6PY) with its Adventure Playground, Smugglers Cove and Carousel. Situated close to J5 of the M25 onto the A21 South it is about 30 minutes from Sevenoaks. There is more about this in the Maidstone chapter but for full details go to www. thehopfarm.co.uk or call 01622 872068

TENTERDEN

The Jewel of the Weald

———◆———

This perfect example of an English country town has a long and distinguished history, having been granted its Royal Charter of Incorporation by King Henry VI in 1449. It grew in prosperity as nearby Small Hythe was the centre of a thriving ship building industry, until the river Rother became silted up after the great storms of the fifteenth century. Even today the town's coat of arms, to be seen on the town sign on the Town Hall balcony and other spots around the town, shows a three masted ship.

'Welcome to Tenterden sign'

The town has long had a tradition for independence and four Tenterden families were on the 'Hercules' which sailed from Sandwich to New England in 1635. The descendent of one of these families, **Samuel Tilden (1814-1886)**, became Governor of New York and a candidate for the Presidency in the 1876 election.

There are also wonderful gardens within a few miles of the town and two of these gardens were rescued from ruins by two different women writers. **Frances Hodgson Burnett's** 'secret garden' is three miles south west of Tenterden, whilst **Vita Sackville-West's** lovely "garden inside a ruin inside a farm" is six miles away. Not to be outdone, some ten miles away H.E.Bates also made a wilderness bloom, as he converted an untamed acre around his house into a place of beauty.

TENTERDEN'S WRITERS

William Caxton (1422-1491)

There is a longstanding tradition that the printer of the first book in English in 1473 was born in the town, although he is also claimed by Hadlow, near Tonbridge. At least it is well documented that his earliest years were spent in the Kentish Weald and that a Thomas Kaxton (conjectured to be a brother) was Tenterden's Town Clerk in 1453-4.

Frances Hodgson Burnett (1849-1924)

Frances was born and brought up in Manchester. After the death of her father her family faced great economic hardship. As so many others did in similar situations in the mid-nineteenth century, they emigrated when Frances was sixteen to America, in their case to Tennessee where her maternal uncle lived.

Once there it was her pen (she was later to describe herself as "a kind of pen-driving machine") that was to bring her great fame and consequently great wealth. This was especially the case once she had produced 'Little Lord Fauntleroy' in 1886. That velvet-collared, long-haired paragon of childhood may not be to the taste of twenty first century readers, but he was exactly what the Victorians wanted.

Frances' personal life, however, was filled with great sadness. One of her two beloved sons died from tuberculosis and her marriage became increasingly unhappy. Almost inevitably there was a divorce and at the age of forty nine she returned to her native country. She had never severed her ties with England and had been making annual visits for a long time.

She leased Great Maytham Hall in Rolveden (three miles from Tenterden) and fell in love with its beautiful walled garden, dating from

1721. She worked tirelessly to rescue the overgrown ruin, planting it with hundreds of roses and setting up a table and chairs in the gazebo, her retreat on rainy days. It was here, always dressed in white and wearing a large hat, where she sat and wrote and, of course, it was the inspiration for her best selling children's novel 'The Secret Garden'.

Although she certainly began writing it in her own secret garden, the final version was largely a product of memory. By 1911, when the novel was published, she had left Rolveden and returned to America. After her death her body was buried in her adopted country with a memorial placed in Rolveden Church.

Joseph Conrad (1857-1924)

This nom de plume is much easier on the English tongue than the Polish writer's true name of Jozef Teodor Konrad Korzeniowski. He lived at a number of places in Kent, the final one being Bishopsbourne outside Canterbury and the memorial stone over his grave in Canterbury cemetery does give his original full name (more information about this is to be found in the Canterbury chapter).

From 1910 to1919 Conrad lived in Capel House, an old farmhouse in the small village of Orlestone, about eight miles from Tenterden. Here he was able to gain some respite from the ill health and depression that so often afflicted him. Twelve years before, whilst still living in Essex, he wrote to a friend about the many bouts of writers' block from which he suffered and the misery these caused him.

"I sit down for eight hours every day and the sitting down is all. In the course of the working day of eight hours I write three sentences, which I erase before leaving the table in despair. Sometimes it takes all my resolution and power of self-control to refrain from butting my head against the wall. I want to howl and foam at the mouth but I daren't do it for fear of waking the baby and alarming my wife."

The move to Kent seems to have brought him peace of mind. He found Orlestone "sympathetic" and was able to write both the long short story 'A Smile of Fortune' and the novels 'Chance' and 'Victory' here.

Vita Sackville-West (1892-1962)

Although she proudly claimed in the 1930s that her thirteenth-great grandfather had once lived at Sissinghurst, it was actually one of those amazing lucky accidents which brought The Hon.Victoria Mary Sackville-West to this part of Kent.

She was the only child of Lord and Lady Sackville of Knole and if she had been a boy she would have inherited that grand house on the outskirts of Sevenoaks. In fact, after her father's death, it was a male cousin who inherited. The loss weighed very heavily on her but Sissinghurst Castle was certainly a tremendous consolation prize. She and her husband, Harold Nicolson, first saw the ruined Elizabethan manor-house on an April day in 1930.

Vita instantly fell in love with the majestic pink brick Tudor gateway, standing in the ruined walled gardens close by the moat. She dubbed it "Sleeping Beauty's Castle". Both buildings and garden were crying out for much tender loving care and it was she who had the vision to see what could be made of it all. Over the next thirty years she and Harold turned "the truly appalling mess of rubbish, old bedsteads and old ploughshares" into one of England's greatest gardens.

'Sissinghurst Castle – Tower'

For the first few nights at Sissinghurst Vita and Harold slept in the tower on camp beds, reading by candlelight. Almost immediately, however, the tower became Vita's sanctuary and hers alone. She used the little room over the arch as her writing room with her desk facing the tapestry landscape on the wall rather than the distracting views of the Kentish Weald outside. In winter the room was icy but she rarely bothered to light a fire. Instead she piled on more and more coats and blankets.

She wrote twenty books in this tower room, including her best known novel 'All Passion Spent' (1931). Her preoccupation with Sissinghurst's lovely garden also meant her literary production changed, so that between 1946 and 1961 she wrote a weekly gardening column for 'The Observer', full of inspirational advice for her readers. Although a much respected author (in 1946 she was appointed Companion of Honour for Services to Literature), it is Sissinghurst garden which remains for many her greatest creative legacy.

The Nicolson Family

Harold Nicolson (1886-1968)

The remaining rooms of the ruined castle were so scattered that Vita, her husband Harold Nicolson and their two sons had separate quarters in different parts of the grounds. Harold made his home in the fifteenth century South Cottage. Here he wrote 'The English Sense of Humour' in 1947 and his 1953 biography of King George V.

'South Cottage home of Harold Nicholson'

In fact it is ironic that although Vita Sackville-West has the reputation of being Sissinghurst's 'Writer in Residence' it was actually her husband, a diplomat as well as a writer, who wrote most words there.

Every morning after breakfast, when his diplomatic duties did not take him abroad, he would write up his diary on one of his three typewriters (Rikki, Tikki and Tavi). Completed diaries were consigned to the filing cabinet: "without thought of publication". It was not until after his parents' deaths that they were edited by Vita and Harold's son **Nigel Nicolson (1917-2004)**. They were published as 'Portrait of a Marriage' and provide an amazing description of this unorthodox relationship.

Today it is the third generation of Nicolsons who inhabit Sissinghurst, as tenants of The National Trust, and they too are continuing the literary tradition. Nigel Nicolson's son, **Adam (1957-)**, has moved here with his wife **Sarah Raven (1963-)** (gardening writer and author of ravishing books on garden design). He is the author of many books about history, travel and the environment and the winner of many prestigious literary prizes. We strongly recommend having a copy of his 'Sissinghurst: An Unfinished History' to hand while you visit.

Try to fit in one of his sister **Juliet Nicolson's** books too. This writer and journalist has written two best selling history books: 'The Perfect Summer, England in 1911' and 'The Great Silence 1918 -1920'. Meanwhile third sibling **Rebecca Nicolson** is the founder and publisher of the fascinating series: 'Short Books'.

H.E. Bates (1905-1974)

The novelist and short story writer Herbert Ernest Bates was born in Northamptonshire but spent the last forty years of his life in Little Chart near Tenterden. He was only absent at times because he was commissioned into the RAF during World War II, with the specific brief to write short stories.

It had become apparent to the Air Ministry that the war effort would be greatly helped if the civilian population could be made aware what life was like on the front line. One realistic story was worth any number of facts and figures when it came to winning hearts and minds. These stirring stories, first published in the 'News Chronicle', were ascribed to Flying Officer X and were later published in book form as, among others, 'How Sleep the Brave'.

Although Bates maintained a prodigious output, averaging one novel and a collection of short stories every year, it is his 1958 best seller, 'The Darling Buds of May' on which his later fame largely rests. The title comes from Shakespeare's sonnet No.18. "Shall I compare thee to a summer's day? / Thou art more lovely and more temperate / Rough winds do shake the darling buds of May" but the inspiration for Pop Larkin and his family was a much more earthy source.

Bates was in his local shop when the real life Pa Larkin came in and pulled out a vast number of old bank notes to treat his trailer load of children with Easter eggs, sweets and ice creams.

They were on holiday from their Wiltshire home - the original Larkin family was not from these parts. After this original inspiration it was the "perfick world" of Kentish villages around Little Chart where Bates lived, which became immortalized in the stories. These stories reached an even wider audience after his death when they were adapted for television by his son Richard.

ONE DAY VISIT

Today you are on the trail of three remarkable women. As the tour also involves two National Trust properties (Small Hythe and Sissinghurst), a little planning is needed. Both are open between 10.30am and 5.00pm from mid-March (late February for Small Hythe) until the end of October. Sissinghurst is closed on Wednesdays and Thursdays while Small Hythe shuts on Thursdays and Fridays. To avoid disappointment it's probably best to avoid those three days if you are making a grand literary tour of the area.

Your first challenge is to find the Tourist Office, located in Tenterden's lovely High Street. Look out for the building called Tenterden Gateway. It's next door to the Post Office so the red post box outside is a good landmark. The building is shared with the library and has plenty of useful information about the area. For more information, go to www.tenterdentown.co.uk or 01580 762558.

'Tenterden Gateway (and Tourist Office)'

If you follow our itinerary you have a tightly packed schedule but if you can spread your sightseeing over more days you should have the luxury of looking round the town museum (closed in winter) in nearby Station Street, off the High Street. The attractive two storey weatherboard building has six floors covering the history of the town from earliest times. More information on the museum can be found at www.tenterdenmuseum.co.uk or 01580 764310.

Also worth finding in the town is a house called Dovenden in Woodchurch Road, still a private residence today. In 1774 it was the home of the **Vineys**, a leading Dissenting family in Kent. They were visited there by two distinguished Americans, the scientist **Joseph Priestley (1703-1804)** and the statesman **Benjamin Franklin (1706-1790)**, who went on to speak at The Meeting House in Ashford Road.

And so to Small Hythe Place (TN30 7NG), the home of the first of today's remarkable women. Before your visit more information is available on 01580 762334 or www.nationaltrust.co.uk/smallhytheplace.

Go south out of Tenterden High Street and turn left by the William Caxton public house on to the B2082, the Rye road. Small Hythe Place is just over two miles along on the left hand side, with free roadside parking a further 50 yards from the house.

'Small Hythe Place'

This half-timbered Elizabethan house was built as a home for the harbour master in the early sixteenth century, when Small Hythe was a thriving shipbuilding area. Three hundred years later, from 1899 until 1928, it was the home of the first of our three remarkable women, Victorian actress **Ellen Terry (1847-1928)** and houses her incredible theatre collection.

Among other treasures are **Alexandre Dumas' (1802-1870)** visiting card, **Sir Arthur Sullivan's (1842-1900)** monocle and a letter from **Oscar Wilde (1854-1900)**, begging Ellen Terry to accept "the first copy of my first play" and hoping that "some day I shall be fortunate enough to write something worthy of your playing".

There is also a theatrical costume exhibition with Ellen Terry's famous beetle-wing dress and many mementos from her leading Shakespearian roles. Interestingly, she once told **Henry Irving (1838-1905)** that Shakespeare was the only man she had ever truly loved.

Refreshments are available from 12.00 noon in the tea room attached to the Barn Theatre, which has a full programme of events, mainly in the summer months.

It's time now for the second remarkable woman, **Vita Sackville-**

West. To find her garden it's probably simplest to retrace your earlier route, leaving Small Hythe and returning to Tenterden. From here it is eight and a half miles to Sissinghurst. Drive the length of the High Street and then take the northbound A262 to Biddenden, about five miles from Tenterden. From here the A262 veers to the left for Sissinghurst. You will find the route well sign-posted. Information for Sissinghurst Castle (TN17 2AB) is available on 01580 710701 or log on to www.nationaltrust. org.uk/sissinghurst.

We recommend you get there in time for lunch. Fruit and vegetables grown on the estate's vegetable garden are used in the restaurant, with meat and eggs being produced by the tenant farmer.

Where does one start to explore the estate? At its heart, both literally and figuratively, is the iconic central tower with Vita's study on the first floor. Up the spiral staircase on the second floor is the printing press used by **Virginia (1882-1941)** and **Leonard Woolf (1880-1969)** to print the first edition of 'The Waste Land' in 1922 and other early works of The Hogarth Press. If you take a deep breath and go up the spiral staircase to The Turret you will find diaries, letters and a fascinating collection of pictures showing the restoration of the house and gardens. There are breathtaking views over the Kentish countryside from the roof.

The gardens are designed as a series of 'rooms' and perhaps the loveliest is the White Garden. Vita died close by here in the Priest's House which was later to become the last home of the poet and novelist **Richard Church (1893-1972)**.

Another writer was there two centuries earlier. In December 1760, when the original Tudor house was still largely intact, the historian and author **Edward Gibbon (1737-1794)** was in residence.

He was then a twenty three year old officer in the Hampshire Militia, which was part of a detachment guarding nearly two thousand French naval prisoners from the Seven Years War. He disliked the whole experience. He wrote in his diary that he was "sick of so hateful a service". He felt that life at Sissinghurst was "at best, not a life for a man of letters". Certainly the French prisoners left their mark on 'Le Chateau de Sissengherst', venting their fury, and boredom, by destroying a great deal of its fabric. The castle's descent into ruin can be dated from that time. In his 2008 book

'Sissinghurst, an Unfinished History', **Adam Nicolson** recounts a fascinating anecdote which brings all this to life.

In the 1930s Vita met a "very old" gentleman who had lived in the Castle in his boyhood. He had been a ten year old in the 1860s when he met a ninety year old labourer, who had been about thirty in 1800. The labourer's father-in-law told him that he "had been employed not only to pull down the walls, but also to pick the foundations in 1763". Now that really is living history. The Library, on your left as you enter the garden, has some fascinating exhibits including a recently acquired contemporary drawing of the French occupation.

When you finally drag yourself away, a short drive will bring you to today's third remarkable woman, **Frances Hodgson Burnett**. After leaving the castle estate turn right to rejoin the A262. Sissinghurst village is one mile east. Another half mile will bring you to a roundabout. Turn left, southbound, onto the A229 for two and a half miles, passing Cranbrook School on the right. **Hammond Innes (1913-1998)**, born over the county boundary in Horsham, Sussex, was a pupil here.

On the left hand side in Cranbrook town centre is the George Hotel. **Edward Gibbon** was billeted at the George Inn (as it was then called) while guarding French prisoners at Sissinghurst. Veer left onto the High Street and after half a mile join the Hatley road. At Hatley join the east bound B2086 to drive six miles to Rolveden.

Drive down Rolveden High Street to the parish church. On the south wall (the far wall opposite the entrance you have just come through) is a memorial plaque to **Frances Hodgson Burnett**. Her body was buried in America. Next, turn off the A28 down Maytham Lane to see the exterior of her home, the magnificent Great Maytham Hall (TN17 4NC), where she lived between 1898 and 1907. **Ellen Terry** visited here from nearby Small Hythe, as did **Henry James (1843-1916)** and **Rudyard Kipling (1865-1936)**. Both men lived just over the border in Sussex.

'Great Maytham Hall gateway arch'

In 1910 the house passed into the ownership of the Rt. Hon. H. J. Tennant, who commissioned Sir Edwin Lutyens to design the present hall, using the original site and incorporating part of the original eighteenth century house. In 1936 the Hall was sold to Thomas Cook of travel fame. Today it is private property and divided up into luxury apartments but the wonderful gardens, remodelled by Lutyens, are opened annually for charity, usually in mid-June when the parkland and walled garden are at their best.

From Great Maytham Hall it is a three mile drive back to Tenterden along the A28 to finish off the day's round trip.

TWO DAY VISIT

Today you are on the trail of two very different novelists who lived in this area. Shortly you will discover H.E. Bates' home and the setting for so many of his stories. One feels as though the sun always shines on the Larkin family but, closer to Tenterden, you can track down where Joseph Conrad's darker vision was first expressed. It's a circular route through

Kentish lanes and very pretty it is too, but with less signposting than on major roads you'd be well advised to allow yourself plenty of time.

It's about eight miles from Tenterden to the nearby home of Joseph Conrad. Drive north up Tenterden High Street and at the village sign veer right onto the B2067, signposted to Woodchurch. Continue along this road making sure you take the left hand turn at the T junction and then almost immediately the right turn, again signposted Woodchurch. You are still on the B2067.

In the centre of Hamstreet turn left onto the Ashford Road. Drive up the hill, under a railway bridge, passing the train station on your right and the primary school on your left. Pass a sign to Orlestone Church on your right then turn right at the unusually named Sugar Loaf Farmhouse down Capel Road. About 100 yards on the left is Capel Cottage and immediately beyond, set back from the road behind a hedge, is the imposing Capel House (TN26 2EH), home to Joseph Conrad between 1910 and 1919.

'Capel Farmhouse'

Return to Sugar Loaf Farmhouse at the end of Capel Road and turn right into Bromley Green for one mile. Turn sharp left into Hornash Road, passing Manor Farm on your right. One mile from Bromley

Green drive through Shadoxhurst and at the village hall turn right into Tally Ho Road, signposted Ashford. At Stubbs Cross T junction turn left to Great Chart and at the next T junction right onto the A28.

You should be 2.75 miles from Shadoxhurst; everything is very close round here. After 200 yards turn left to Great Chart. Drive down The Street, past the delightfully named pub Hoodeners Horse with the Swan on the left. Turn left at Ninn Lane (signposted Hothfield). After a mile it becomes Etchden Road.

After half a mile turn right into Bear's Lane for just less than a mile and then turn right into Bethersden. After a mile you will come into The Street at Hothfield. It's about five miles from that original turning into Ninn's Lane.

Head North along The Street for 300 yards and turn left onto West Street, which soon becomes Swan Lane. After a mile and a half turn right into Ram Lane. In a few hundred yards this leads to Little Chart Forstal. You have reached your destination (TN27 0PU).

'The Granary at Little Chart Forstal'

This picture postcard village was home to H.E. Bates and his wife Madge for more than forty years. In 1931 they found a derelict old granary overlooking the village green. It then became a labour of love for them both to convert it into a home, where they were to bring up two sons and two daughters. He was a very keen and knowledgeable gardener and turned the acre of rough ground surrounding their home into a dramatic riot of colour and wrote several gardening books while doing so.

After his death in 1974 Madge moved into a bungalow, which had originally been a cow byre, next to the Granary. She died there in 2004 aged 95.

When you leave Little Chart you might want to see where 'The Darling Buds of May' was filmed for TV. It's only a mile and a half from there.

Return to Swan Lane and turn right down the hill passing a church on your left and the Swan Inn on your right. Continue on Swan Lane for a mile until you get to The Street at Pluckley. Although, like all the lovely villages round here, it looks so idyllic, it actually claims to be the most haunted village in England, with at least twelve spooky apparitions calling this home.

At the time of writing this guide there is free street parking here. If you are feeling energetic you could arm yourself with the AA walk, 'Orchards and Perfick Villages Around Pluckley', for a gentle three mile ramble. It takes in Pluckley where the T.V. series was filmed (giving Catherine Zeta Jones her first real starring role) and then back to Little Chart Forstal. The grid reference for the start and finish of the walk is at TQ927454 and the suggested map is OS Explorer 137 or Landranger 189.

Pluckley was also home to the Dering family. The first Baronet, **Sir Edward Dering (1598-1644)**, gave his name to the Dering Manuscript, the earliest extant manuscript text of any Shakespeare play. This version of both parts of Henry IV was discovered here at the family home of Surrenden Manor.

You are on the outskirts of the other large town in the area - Ashford. This market town was the birthplace of **Frederick Forsyth (1938-)**. As a young man he stood on the platform of Ashford station and watched what looked like cloned businessmen, all dressed in identikit dark suits and white shirts, going off to their London offices. He vowed then that he would never become a "penguin" like them and so entered what he felt was the much more individualistic world of journalism and then novel writing.

There's a much more direct route back to Tenterden. Head east from Pluckley along The Street towards Little Chart and after half a mile turn right into Bethersden Road. After two miles turn right and carry on for a further mile and a half continuing then onto Mill Road for three hundred yards. At the junction with The Street and Forge Hill take the left hand fork to Forge Hill and in 300 yards you will reach the A28. Turn right in the direction of Tenterden and then the road does all the hard work for you. Just stay on the same road passing through High Halden and St Michael's and in six miles you will reach Tenterden.

IF YOU HAVE MORE TIME

There is more about H.E. Bates at the Museum of Kentish Life at Maidstone.

Here among many serious displays on farming in the county are several reconstructions: Ma's kitchen and Pop's strawberry shed are our favourites, as well as an exhibition about H.E. Bates himself. Have a look at the Maidstone chapter for more details of this nice day out.

CAN I DO THESE TOURS WITHOUT A CAR?

If you are planning a visit using public transport it's probably best to visit www.travelinesoutheast.org.uk or 0871 2002233 for information beforehand.

There are regular bus services to Tenterden from Ashford, Hastings, Headcorn, Maidstone, Rye and Tunbridge Wells and the train services from London and the South East connect with the bus routes.

The nearest mainline stations are Ashford International, Headcorn and Hastings. Taxis are available in Tenterden for the last part of your journey so with some determination and ingenuity you should be able to see a good deal.

BEST TIME TO VISIT

'H.E. Bates' Country' is at its most "perfick" in the first two weeks in May when the apple blossom is out. Many would say it's the best time to see the best part of the best county in England.

IF YOU HAVE CHILDREN

It is possible to have a fun day out from your base in Tenterden which will appeal to accompanying children and also help you track down some literary sites.

The Kent and East Sussex Steam Railway advertises itself as "England's Finest Light Railway". From Tenterden Town Station (close to Tenterden museum), the ten miles of track go through Rolveden and eventually over the Kent/East Sussex border to Bodiam castle. With advance booking you can even collect a picnic hamper at Tenterden Town Station. More information is available on www.kest.org.uk or 01580 765155.

While you are on the H.E. Bates trail you will make the young back seat passengers very happy with a trip to Port Lympne. This wild animal park near Ashford (Exit 11 off the M20, south of Ashford) has the largest herd of black rhino outside Africa and the world's largest Gorillarium, as well as many more species, including lions, tigers and giraffe. More information on www.aspinallfoundation.org or 1844 8424647.

In the same area we would strongly recommend The Rare Breeds Centre (TN26 3RJ) on the B2067, between Hamstreet and Woodchurch, with its friendly farm animals, woodland assault course, butterfly tunnel and much more.

TAILPIECE – MEET the TEAM

Two like-minded couples sharing a passion for literature and travel. Following writers is their idea of heaven.

Judith Bastide - the principal author, was Head of English at a prestigious South Coast girls school (famous Old Girls include actress Prunella Scales and writer Rumer Godden). Judith is an enthusiastic literary detective who has dragged her long suffering husband and family around the county, tracking its writers. This book should make it easier for fellow addicts.

Michael Rich - a retired dentist and an avid reader, he was the collator of the various book chapters. He did proof reading, main editing of the text and corrected typos. He was responsible for liaising with the publishers, taking the photographs, the website and all other IT work.

Derek Bastide - a former university lecturer and currently school inspector with many books and articles to his credit. This book would never have been possible without his navigational skills driving his wife, Judith, through the country lanes of Kent. We are very grateful!

Gillian Rich - a mathematician and former school librarian. She is the author of several maths text books and is involved with online publishing, as well as being passionate about the arts. Gillian was the originator of this project.

INDEX of people

A

Ainsworth Harrison, 106
Anderson Hans Christian, 68, 105
Andy Pandy, 138, 139, 150
Arnold Mathew, 27
Atterbury Audrey, 139
Austen Jane, 14, 15, 17, 67, 109, 124,
    127, 128, 141

B

Ballantyne R.M., 68
Barham Richard Harris, 8, 43, 66
Barrie J.M., 39
Bates H.E., 81, 164, 170, 172, 174, 175
Bear Rupert, 7, 13, 21
'Beau' Nash Richard, 120
Becket St. Thomas a, 1, 9, 15
Behn Aphra, x, 16
Belloc Hilaire, 39
Bennett Arnold, 39
Bestall Alfred, 7
Betjeman John, 64
Bird Maria, 138, 150

Blake William, 151
Bolt Robert, 12
Bond James, x, 6, 16, 25, 30, 31, 33
Bowen Elizabeth, 57
Brooke Jocelyn, 7, 46
Brown Ford Madox, 53, 65
Buchan John, 57
Burnett Frances Hodgson, 160, 169
Burney Fanny, 39, 115, 120
Butler Samuel, 152
Byron Lord, 23

C

Carroll Lewis, 148
Caxton William, 160, 166
Chagall Marc, 125
Charles II, 16, 94
Chaucer Geoffrey, 1, 13
Churchill Sir Winston, 135, 147, 149
Church Richard, 133, 168
Cobbett William, 42, 102
Coghill Nevill, 18
Coleridge Samuel Taylor, 67

Collins Wilkie, 24, 28, 59, 67, 105
Conrad Joseph, 6, 8, 13, 25, 45, 108,
    161, 170, 171. *See* Korzeniowski
    Joseph
Coward Noel, 25, 29, 30, 42, 44
Crompton Lamburn Richmal, 154
Cumberland Richard, 115, 122

D

Darnley Lord, 109
Darwin Charles, 152
Davies W.H., 137, 146
Defoe Daniel, 32, 55, 106, 114
Dering Sir Edward, 173
Dickens Charles, ix, 9, 10, 24, 28, 35,
    52, 54, 55, 63, 68, 80, 82, 87, 90,
    98, 100, 103, 107, 142
Dickens John, 88, 89, 90, 102, 103, 104
Disraeli Benjamin, 71
Donne John, 142, 143
Doyle Conan, 129, 130
Drayton Michael, 143
Dryden John, 144
Dumas Alexandre, 167
Dunsany Lord, 151

E

Edward III, 2
Eliot George, 28
Eliot T.S., 9, 20, 63
Elizabeth I, Queen, 3, 4, 61, 143
Eliza Lynn. *See* Linton Eliza Lynn
Erasmus, 15, 44
Evelyn John, 121, 130, 132

F

Fermore Sir Patrick Leigh, 6
Firmin Peter, 54
Fleming Ann, 33
Fleming Ian, x, 16, 25, 30
Fletcher John, 143
Ford Madox Ford, 45
Forster E.M., 118, 123, 128
Forsyth Frederick, 118, 128, 173

Franklin Benjamin, 166
Frizer Ingram, 4
Frost Robert, 74
Fryth John, 147

G

Galsworthy John, 39
Garnett David, 137
Garnett Edward, 137
Gaunt John of, 2
George III, 63
Gibbon Edward, 168, 169
Gogh Vincent van, 66
Golding William, 83
Graves Robert, 124

H

Hamilton Charles, 53
Hansard Luke, 148
Hasted Edward, 100
Hazlitt William, 73, 75
Henry VIII, 72
Hill Octavia, 156
Hooker Richard, 7, 45
Hugo Victor, 47

I

Ingoldsby Thomas, 8, 43
Innes Hammond, 169
Irving Henry, 167

J

Jacobs W.W., 32
James Henry, 25, 38, 169
James M.R., 17
Jonson Ben, 132, 143

K

Kean Edmund, 119
Keats John, 63
Keyes Sidney, 118, 128
Kipling Rudyard, 39, 169
Korzeniowski Joseph, 6, 8, 13, 25, 45,

108, 161, 170, 171. *See* Conrad
Joseph

L

Lamb Lady Caroline, 23
Lawrence D.H., 61
Lewis Sinclair, 78
Liddell Alice, 148
Lingstrom Freda, 138, 139, 150
Linton Eliza Lynn, 105. *See* Lynn Eliza
Lovelace Richard, 13
Lushington Edmund, 81
Lyly John, 3, 9
Lynn Dame Vera, 23
Lynn Eliza, 105. *See* Linton Eliza
    Lynn

M

Marlowe Christopher, x, 1, 3, 8, 9, 10,
    16
Marx Jenny, 68
Marx Karl, 68
Mate Charles, 63
Maugham Rev'd. Henry MacDonald,
    5
Maugham Somerset, x, 3, 5, 10, 16
More Thomas, 12
Muir Frank, 66

N

Nesbit Edith, 29, 41, 42, 151
Nicolson Adam, 169
Nicolson Harold, 133, 137, 144, 162,
    163
Nicolson Juliet, 164
Nicolson Nigel, 164
Nicolson Rebecca, 164
North, Lord Dudley, 113

O

Oldcastle Sir John, 101
Orczy Baroness, 66, 79
Orwell George, 77
Owen Wilfred, 47

P

Paine Tom, 32
Palmer Samuel, 151
Parr-Byrne Lesley, 62
Pepys Samuel, 121, 144
Pocahontas, 108
Postgate Oliver, 54, 58, 69
Powell Anthony, 152
Priestley Joseph, 166
Prior Matthew, 144

R

Raven Sarah, 164
Raverat Gwen, 152
Richards Frank, 53
Rossetti Christina, 53
Rossetti Dante Gabriel, 53, 65

S

Sackville Charles, 143, 144
Sackville Sir Thomas, 143
Sackville-West Vita, 133, 137, 144, 160,
    161, 164, 168
Sassoon Siegfried, 117, 124, 134
Sayers Dorothy L., 9
Seth Vikram, 118, 128
Seton Anya, 154
Shadwell Thomas, 144
Shakespeare William, 3, 4, 26
Shaw George Bernard, 39, 61, 63
Shelley Mary, 24, 39
Siddons Sarah, 39, 63
Sidney Sir Philip, 129, 132
Smart Chistopher, 83
Smith Horace, 123
Streatfeild Noel, 147
Strong Mary Pearson, 58
Sullivan Sir Arthur, 167
Swynford Katherine, 2

T

Tennyson Lord Alfred, 80
Ternan Ellen, 35, 82, 90

Terry Ellen, 167, 169
Thackeray William Makepeace, 28, 116, 123
Theroux Paul, 32
Thomas Edward, 73, 78, 136, 145
Thorndike Dame Sybil, 95
Thorndike Russell, 40, 41, 95
Thrale Hester, 120
Tilden Samuel, 159
Tourtel Mary, 7
Tyler Wat, 71, 77

V

Voysey C.F., 25, 38

W

Waal Edmund de, 6
Waller Edmund, 129, 131
Walpole Hugh, 3, 6
Walsingham Sir Francis, 3
Walton Izaak, 13
Washington George, 76
Washington Laurence, 76

Waterstone Tim, 118, 128
Watts Richard, 91, 97
Wells H.G., 25, 37, 48, 153
Wiat Sir Francis, 81
Widdecombe Ann, 72
Wilde Oscar, 167
Woolf Leonard, 168
Woolf Virginia, 144
Wyatt Thomas, 72, 81

Z

Zborowski Count Louis, 25, 33